The Essential Guide to Macramé for Beginners

Mastering the Art of Handcrafted Home Decor and Gift Ideas

Alexandra Dixon Jackson

UNLOCK THE POWER OF MACRAMÉ

Exclusive Resource Hub

Congratulations on getting your hands on
"The Essential Guide to Macramé for Beginners"!

As a token of my appreciation,
I've curated a **LIBRARY OF RESOURCES**
including video tutorials and helpful guides, that will take
your macramé skills from beginner to master!

Here's what you can expect to find inside:

1. Master the essential **macramé knots**,
from foundation to advanced techniques
2. Discover the secrets to creating stunning,
one-of-a-kind **patterns and designs**
3. Dive into **beginner-friendly projects**
that will build your skills and confidence in no time
4. Explore the library for helpful
downloadable guides and printable resources.

Scan the QR code found on the last page of the book.
Don't miss out — unlock your rewards today!

Table of Contents

Introduction

Welcome to the wonderful world of macramé, my fellow creative adventurer! If this book has found its way into your hands, something truly magical is about to unfold. Now, macramé is my heart's desire, not merely a pastime; it has encapsulated my soul since childhood, has charmed my heart, and has guided my life's path. And today, I am honored to share the ancient wonders of this exquisite craft with you.

Imagine not only decorating your space with beautiful, handmade creations but also infusing it with a piece of your heart and soul. Whether you're seeking a creative outlet, desiring to add a personal touch to your home, or looking for a heartfelt gift, macramé is your answer. And I'm here to guide you every step of the way, ensuring that you master the art of knotting with ease and joy.

Allow me to introduce myself. I am Alexandra Dixon Jackson, your macramé mentor and companion on this exciting journey. Born under the azure sky of Turkey, I've had the fortune of embracing a rich cultural heritage that has indelibly impacted my passion for the artistic. At the tender age of fifteen, I migrated to the bustling city of New York, where my passion for macramé truly ignited. It began with treasured recollections of my grandmother's intricate, knotted art, and it has now blossomed into my life's mission to share this age-old craft with creative souls like you.

As you commence this exciting adventure, remember that macramé is a skill that anyone can master with guidance and practice. In the following chapters, I will hold your hand and lead you through the fundamentals, ensuring you have a solid foundation.

Before diving into the transformative process, let's ensure you've assembled the necessary tools and spaces that fuel your creativity. I'll share my tried-and-tested secrets for setting up an economical, clutter-free sanctuary that nurtures your artistic spirit.

Next, penetrate the core of macramé – the materials. From the earthy charm of hemp and jute to the sleek sophistication of nylon and more, I'll demystify the vibrant spectrum of macramé cord options. Together, we'll conquer the best choices for your masterpiece, balancing style, durability, and sustainability.

Once you've chosen your perfect cord companion, it's time to untangle the mysteries of macramé measurements. I'll spill Macramé's inner-secrets to ensure you never fall short again. I'll also share my macramé math pro-tips to help you plan like a pro and never run out of cord. And should accidents happen (because they sometimes do), my quick-fix guide will save the day, untangling any messy mishaps.

There's no time to waste – it's time to get knotty! I'll be your virtual, hand-holding assistant as we navigate the essentials knots, such as the Lark's Head Knot and Square Knot, which serve as the building blocks for your macramé journey. There's a rich tapestry of possibilities with these knots, trust me! We'll also uncover special knots that will add texture and dimension to your pieces, making your creations truly stand out. You'll be amazed at the countless design possibilities when you master these essential knots.

With practice comes confidence, and soon, you'll be able to experiment with mounting techniques, textures, and even adding sparkly embellishments like beads and tassels. Watch your confidence soar as your skillset expands and your artistic voice unfolds.

Finally, we'll tackle the inevitable – the freak out-worthy troubleshooting chapter. Don't worry, we've all been there. I've thoroughly covered this chapter with quick fixes and expert-approved pro-tips to remedy any macramé mishap. Rest assured, my years of experience and countless half-finished projects have prepared me to guide you through any challenge.

But this book is not a series of tutorials and projects. It's a journey of self-discovery, a celebration of creativity, and a reminder that you are capable of more than you imagine. It's about embracing your creativity, trusting your instincts, and celebrating your uniqueness. It's about recognizing that imperfection is beauty and that mistakes are opportunities. Each chapter is thoughtfully crafted to empower you with the knowledge and confidence to succeed. As you work through these pages, I want you to remember that macramé is a process, not a product. It's about the joy of creating, the thrill of learning, and the sense of pride that comes with making something with your own two hands.

As you venture forth on this transformative journey with me, I want you to embrace the notion that you're not just learning a new skill – you're cultivating a sense of self-love, self-acceptance, and self-expression. You are giving yourself the gift of time to slow down, breathe, and find peace in the act of creation.

So, take a deep breath, dear reader, and let's begin. Let's untangle the threads of doubt and uncertainty, and weave a tapestry of confidence, creativity, and connection. Let's create something truly remarkable – not just a piece of macramé, but a reflection of our true selves.

From this point onward, I'll share my must-have secrets, my tips, and my passion for this noble craft. But most importantly, I'll share my heart, my enthusiasm, and my belief in you. Because I know, together, we can create something truly extraordinary – a world of beauty, a world of love, and a world of handmade magic.

With warmth and fondness,
Alexandra

Chapter 1: Welcome to Macramé

1.1 What is Macramé?

Welcome, my craft-loving companion, to the fascinating world of macramé! Prepare to set forth on a creative quest that will not only ignite your imagination but also equip you to craft stunning pieces that will inspire pride and admiration. So, what exactly is macramé, and why is everyone talking about it? Simply put, macramé is the art of tying knots in a decorative way to create stunning textiles. It's like friendship bracelets on steroids! With just a few simple tools and some cord, you can craft everything from wall hangings and plant hangers to jewelry and bags. But here's the real kicker: macramé is incredibly easy to learn. You don't need to be a crafting pro or have any special skills to get started. If you can tie a knot, you can macramé! And the best part? The satisfaction of creating something beautiful with your own two hands is unbeatable.

Macramé is more than just a trend; it's a creative outlet that allows you to express your unique style. Whether you're into bohemian vibes, modern minimalism, or anything in between, there's a macramé project that will speak to your soul. Plus, it's a great way to add a personal touch to your home decor or create one-of-a-kind gifts for your loved ones.

The world of macramé is vast and diverse, offering a range of styles and techniques for craft enthusiasts to undertake. By tracing the origins of macramé, you will stumble upon the traditional styles that have been handed down through generations. These classic techniques often involve intricate knotting patterns and designs, creating beautiful decorative pieces such as wall hangings, plant hangers, and curtains. Traditional macramé embodies a sense of timelessness and craftsmanship that is cherished by many artisans. Types of macramé have evolved over time, incorporating contemporary elements and innovative approaches. Modern macramé embraces experimentation with materials, colors, and styles, pushing the boundaries of what was once considered traditional. Jewelry making has also found a place in macramé, with artisans crafting intricate necklaces, bracelets, and earrings using knotting techniques. The delicate balance of beauty and skill required in creating macramé jewelry adds a touch of elegance to any ensemble.

But beyond the aesthetic appeal, there's something deeply therapeutic about the rhythmic process of tying knots. It's like meditation for your hands! As you focus on each knot, the stresses of daily life seem to melt away, leaving you feeling centered and calm. And when you step back to admire your finished project, you'll feel a sense of pride and accomplishment that's hard to beat.

1.2 History and Origins of Macramé

Just like the intricate knots that make up this beautiful craft, the history of macramé is intertwined with cultures and traditions around the world. Believe it or not, the earliest known origins of macramé date back to the 13th century, when Arab weavers used intricate knotting techniques to create beautiful textiles and decorative items.

Ancient cultures, such as the Babylonians and Assyrians, employed knotting methods to design elaborate fabrics and ornate embellishments. As trade routes expanded, the art of macramé spread far and wide, finding its way to Europe during the Age of Exploration in the 15th and 16th centuries. Sailors played a significant role in the proliferation of macramé, using their time at sea to create knotted belts, hammocks, and other practical items. These seafaring craftsmen even used macramé to make decorative embellishments for their ships!

Fast forward to the Victorian era, and macramé experienced a surge in popularity as a fashionable pastime for ladies. Drawing rooms across Europe were filled with women creating intricate macramé lace, tablecloths, and other delicate household items. It was during this time that macramé began to be recognized as a true art form, with books and patterns being published to guide aspiring knotters.

In the 1970s, macramé had its groovy moment in the spotlight as a beloved craft of the bohemian set. Hanging planters, wall hangings, and even clothing adorned with macramé knots became iconic symbols of the free-spirited, earthy aesthetic of the era. Macramé provided a creative outlet and a means of self-expression for a generation seeking to connect with their artistic side.

While the 1970s saw a surge in macramé popularity, the art form has experienced a renaissance in recent years, making its mark in contemporary art and fashion. Modern artists and designers are pushing the boundaries of traditional macramé techniques, creating innovative and intricate pieces that blur the line between craft and fine art. In the world of fashion, macramé is making a bold statement with stylish accessories and wearable art pieces that celebrate the beauty of handmade craftsmanship.

Considering all points, it is clear that the saga of macramé has been a captivating one, with its roots tracing back centuries to ancient cultures and its resurgence in recent decades. Throughout the ages, macramé has woven a timeless tale of creativity and craftsmanship, captivating the imagination and skilled hands of artisans worldwide. Macramé is sure to remain a beloved artistic expression for many years to come, motivating new generations to uncover the potential of knotting and weaving with cords. As we immerse ourselves in the captivating realm of knots and creativity, we become part of this rich history, adding our own unique chapter to the ever-evolving story of macramé.

1.3 Popularity and Modern Revival

As you take a closer look at the latest trends, you might have noticed that macramé is suddenly everywhere, enjoying a remarkable revival in popularity. This nostalgic craft has seemingly burst onto the scene, capturing the attention of many. But what's driving this renewed interest? What factors have contributed to macramé's widespread appeal? Let's scrutinize the potential rationales and dissect the narrative behind this artistic phenomenon together!

First off, I think it's safe to say that we're all craving a little more authenticity and natural beauty in our lives. Amidst the sea of sameness and uniformity that surrounds us, there's something so refreshing about a handmade piece that showcases the artist's unique touch. Macramé, with its intricate knots and organic fibers, fits that bill perfectly. It's a celebration of craftsmanship and individuality, and that's something we can all appreciate.

Another reason why macramé is having a moment? It's incredibly versatile! Macramé's adaptability is one of its greatest strengths - it can seamlessly infuse a room with unique character. Whether you're seeking to inject a free-spirited essence into a living space or introduce tactile depth to a sleek, modern bedroom, macramé offers a flexible solution. From incorporating statement wall pieces and whimsical plant displays to adding textured accents to furniture and lighting fixtures, the possibilities for creative expression are virtually limitless. With its capacity to blend with various styles and settings, macramé has become a favorite among both professional designers and DIY enthusiasts for its versatility and boundless potential.

But macramé isn't just a pretty face - it's also a fantastic way to bring a sense of warmth and coziness into your home. Those soft, fluffy fibers and intricate knots have a way of making any space feel more inviting and comfortable. As we adjust to a new routine of increased at-home workdays and leisure time, that's a valuable asset. With the intricate knots and corded elegance of macramé, you can turn your home into a tranquil oasis, where the stresses of everyday life melt away, and the soothing essence of this ancient craft transports you to a state of deep serenity and unwinding.

Certainly, discussing the resurgence of macramé necessitates acknowledging the impact of social media. Platforms such as Instagram and Pinterest have been instrumental in introducing this art form to new generations. The visual appeal of these sites offers a perfect platform for macramé creators and aficionados to showcase their work, thereby inspiring a broader audience to take the initiative and try their hand at the craft themselves. With the use of hashtags and sharing features, macramé tutorials and finished pieces can easily reach a large audience, sparking interest and fueling the trend further. It's been incredible to watch the macramé movement grow and evolve in real-time, with new patterns, techniques, and ideas emerging every day.

The modern resurgence of macramé can be linked to the growing interest in DIY crafting and the inclination towards a more eco-conscious lifestyle. As consumers increasingly recognize the environmental footprint of mass-produced goods, they are increasingly seeking out handmade and sustainable alternatives that reduce waste and promote a more mindful approach to consumerism. Macramé fits perfectly into this ethos, as it requires minimal materials and can be made using sustainable fibers like cotton or jute.

But what's the catalyst that's making macramé so trendy at the moment? It's just plain fun! This tactile craft offers a unique way to express oneself creatively, allowing individuals to unwind and tap into their artistic side. The soothing repetitive motions of knot-tying have a meditative quality, capable of calming the mind and promoting mental well-being. Moreover, macramé is an accessible and affordable hobby that requires minimal initial investment, making it easy to get started. As skill levels improve, the possibilities for growth and experimentation expand, fostering a sense of accomplishment and satisfaction. Ultimately, macramé is a creative outlet that embodies the joy of crafting, the thrill of discovery, and the comfort of communal connection.

So, there you have it - just a few of the reasons why macramé is making such a big comeback. This noteworthy trend celebrates the beauty of handmade craftsmanship, the diversity of creative expression, and the simple pleasure of immersing oneself in an art form. And the best part? It's an inclusive movement that invites everyone to participate, regardless of skill level or artistic background, and reap the rewards of a fulfilling and enjoyable hobby.

Chapter 2: Your Macramé Starter Toolkit

The simplicity of DIY macramé is one of its greatest attractions. Unlike other crafts, you don't require a vast array of materials or extensive experience to get started. This accessibility has contributed to its enduring popularity, as it offers a budget-friendly and practical creative outlet that can be tailored to your skill level. Before we launch into our macramé project, let's take a closer look at the basic tools you'll need. You won't need extensive equipment or a fully equipped studio to begin. With a limited set of fundamental supplies, you'll be well-prepared to create intricate and beautiful macramé pieces that showcase your creativity and skill.

2.1 Essential Tools Every Beginner Needs

First up, let's talk about the star of the show: the macramé **board**. This handy little tool is going to be your best friend throughout your exploration of macramé. It typically consists of a sturdy board with evenly spaced holes or pins where you can secure your cords while working on your design. The board provides a stable surface for knotting and allows you to maintain even tension throughout your project.

Using a macramé board can help you create intricate patterns and designs by keeping your cords organized and preventing tangling. It also makes the process of macramé more enjoyable and efficient, giving you a designated space to work on your projects without worrying about them unraveling.

You can find macramé boards in various sizes, so choose one that best suits the scale of your projects. Some boards also come with additional features like measuring guides and clips to hold your cords in place.

Now, in addition to the board, there are a few other types of support equipment that can come in handy:

- Macramé Frame: a wooden or metal frame that can hold your work in place while you knot.
- Macramé Rack: a stand with dowels or hooks to support your work as you create intricate designs.
- Tension Rod: a customizable rod that can be adjusted to hold your macramé piece at the desired height and tension.
- Macramé Wall Hanging Kit: a complete set that includes all the necessary hardware to hang your finished piece on the wall.

Investing in a quality macramé board is a wise decision for any beginner looking to improve their skill and create professional-looking pieces. If you're feeling extra crafty, you can even make your own using a piece of wood and some nails!

Next, you'll need a good pair of **scissors**. Trust me; you don't want to be wrestling with dull or flimsy scissors when you're trying to create intricate knots and patterns. Many beginners underestimate the importance of using sharp scissors when they start to dabble in the craft of macramé. Sharp scissors are important for achieving clean cuts on cords and preventing fraying, which can disrupt the integrity of your macramé projects. Invest in a sharp, comfortable pair that's dedicated solely to your macramé projects. This way, you'll always have them on hand, and they'll stay in tip-top shape.

With respect to choosing scissors for macramé, there are a few key factors to consider. Firstly, opt for scissors that are specifically designed for cutting fabric or crafting materials. These types of scissors are typically sharp enough to cut through various cord thicknesses without causing fraying. Look for scissors with a comfortable grip that fits well in your hand, as you will be using them for extended periods during your macramé projects. Additionally, consider the size of the scissors. While larger scissors may seem more powerful, they can be cumbersome and difficult to maneuver when making intricate cuts in macramé. A medium-sized pair of scissors with pointed tips is often the most versatile option for macramé projects, allowing you to make precise cuts with ease. Take the time to research and choose a reliable brand known for producing durable and sharp scissors that are suitable for macramé. Recognizing the importance of selecting the right pair of scissors will set you up for success in your macramé projects.

Now, let's discuss the importance of measuring tools in your crafting endeavors. Achieving precision and attention to detail is crucial for realizing your artistic ideas. To ensure your projects meet your standards, you'll want to have a **measuring tape** or ruler nearby. When starting a new project, the first step is to measure the length of cord you need. As you progress with your macramé skills, you'll find that measuring tape is also handy for spacing out knots and creating symmetrical designs. By measuring distances between knots or rows, you can maintain consistency and balance throughout your work. This attention to detail will elevate the overall look of your macramé creations and showcase your craftsmanship. With patience and precision, you'll soon master the art of measuring tape and take your macramé skills to the next level.

Concerning precision cutting in macramé, a **rotary cutter** can be a game-changer. This tool features a sharp, circular blade that allows you to glide through cords with ease, resulting in clean and accurate cuts every time. If you're working on projects that require intricate detailing or precise angles, a rotary cutter is a must-have addition to your toolkit.

When opting for a rotary cutter, look for one with a comfortable grip and an adjustable blade. This will give you the flexibility to switch between different cutting depths depending on the thickness of your cords. Additionally, opt for a rotary cutter with safety features such as a locking mechanism to keep the blade secure when not in use. This will prevent any accidents and ensure a smooth cutting experience.

The advantages of using a rotary cutter for your macramé projects are plentiful. Not only does it provide clean and precise cuts, but it also saves you time and effort compared to using traditional scissors. With the ability to cut through multiple layers of cord at once, a rotary cutter streamlines the cutting process and allows you to focus on the creative aspects of your macramé work.

In terms of adding those perfect finishing touches to your macramé projects, **combs and brushes** are imperative tools in your arsenal. A comb is perfect for straightening out fringes, untangling cords, and creating clean lines in your designs. A brush, on the other hand, is ideal for fluffing up fringe and giving your pieces a textured look. With these tools, you can achieve that professional finish that sets your macramé creations apart. Start by combing through your fringes with a comb to ensure they are all straight and even. This will give your project a neat and tidy appearance. Then, use a brush to fluff up the fringe and add texture to your design. You can also use the brush to separate and define individual cords for a more intricate look. These simple steps can make a big difference in the overall appearance of your macramé piece. Mastery of combs and brushes in macramé requires repetitive practice. Take the initiative to experiment with varied techniques and don't hesitate to think outside the box. With persistence and dedication, you'll eventually cultivate a signature approach to utilize these tools and amplify your creative vision.

Another imperative tool for macramé artists is the humble **crochet hook**. While traditionally used for knitting and crocheting, a crochet hook can also be a valuable tool for creating complex knots and intricate designs in macramé. Its small, hook-shaped tip allows you to manipulate cords with ease, making it perfect for working with fine details. With a crochet hook, you can easily create lark's head knots, picot knots, and other decorative knots that add depth and interest to your macramé projects. You can also use a crochet hook to weave in loose ends and tidy up your work, giving your creations a clean and professional finish. Think of it as a magic wand that can elevate your macramé from simple to stunning! Once you master the art of using a crochet hook in macramé, you'll wonder how you ever lived without it.

To keep your cords tangle-free and organized, consider investing in a **cord dispenser**. This nifty tool allows you to easily pull out the length of cord you need without any fuss. Simply place your spools of cord on the dispenser and let it do the work for you. This will save you time and frustration during your macramé projects, allowing you to focus on perfecting your knots and designs. When working on intricate patterns that require multiple cord colors or types, a cord dispenser becomes even more invaluable. You can switch between cords seamlessly, without having to untangle them each time. This not only speeds up your workflow but also ensures a neater finished product. Your cord dispenser will soon become an imperative part of your macramé toolkit, making your projects more enjoyable and efficient. Choose a cord dispenser that suits your workspace and the size of your cords. Whether you opt for a wall-mounted dispenser or a tabletop version, make sure it can accommodate your most commonly used cord spools. With this simple addition to your crafting setup, it's as if you'll have your own personal assistant, always ready to lend a helping hand.

While macramé is primarily about knotting techniques, there are instances where using additional tools like **glue**, a **needle**, and **thread** can enhance the structural integrity of your projects. If you're creating intricate patterns or working with delicate fibers, securing the ends of your cords with a dab of glue can prevent them from unraveling over time. This extra step ensures that your hard work lasts for years to come.

A needle and thread can also come in handy when adding embellishments or attaching different macramé pieces together. You can easily sew small details onto your work or join sections seamlessly for a polished look. Whether you're a beginner or experienced crafter, having these tools at your disposal expands your creative possibilities and allows you to experiment with new techniques. Note, the goal is to savor the process of creating macramé art, so don't be afraid to investigate various tools and techniques to refine your projects. By incorporating glue, a needle, and thread into your toolkit, you're investing in the longevity and versatility of your macramé creations. Enlist these additional tools as allies in your creative pursuit, and witness your skills and designs blossom.

As far as securing your macramé project, cork pads and pins are your best friends. **Cork pads** not only protect your surfaces but also provide a stable base for your work. To use cork pads, simply place them under your project to prevent it from slipping and sliding while you work. This will give you more control over your knots and ensure a clean, finished look. Next, **pins** come in handy for holding your work in place as you progress. Use them to secure loose ends or sections of your project to maintain tension and prevent undoing your hard work. Simply pin down the areas you want to keep in place, making it easier to focus on the next steps of your design. By incorporating cork pads and pins into your macramé toolkit, you'll find that your projects are not only more manageable but also have a cleaner, more professional finish.

S-hooks are a macramé artist's best friend. These versatile tools are perfect for hanging your macramé creations during the finishing touches. You can easily hook your project onto an S-hook and hang it from a rod or rack, allowing you to step back and admire your work as you add final details. S-hooks are also great for organizing your cords and keeping them tangle-free. Simply hang different cords on separate S-hooks to prevent them from getting tangled or knotted, making your work much more efficient. Additionally, you can use S-hooks to display your finished pieces or even store them neatly when not in use. Overall, S-hooks are not only practical but also a stylish addition to your macramé toolkit. By incorporating them into your workflow, you'll find that your projects are easier to manage and your workspace more organized.

Speaking of cords, you'll need something to keep them tidy and organized. A small **storage box** or **basket** is perfect for this purpose. You can easily store your cords, beads, and other accessories, keeping them within reach and ready to use whenever inspiration strikes. You can opt for a sturdy storage box with compartments that allow you to separate your cords by color or length. This will make it easier for you to find the cord you need for your next project without any hassle. Alternatively, you can choose a basket with handles for easy portability, allowing you to take your macramé supplies with you wherever you go. When deciding on a storage box or basket, make sure to consider the size of your cords and the quantity you have. You'll want a container that can comfortably hold all your cords without squishing them together. Additionally, look for a box or basket that is durable and easy to clean, ensuring that your cords remain in good condition for future projects.

By keeping your cords neatly organized in a designated storage box or basket, you'll save time and frustration searching for the right cord. Plus, it adds a touch of organization to your crafting space, making it a more enjoyable experience each time you sit down to create.

Lastly, don't forget about **lighting**! Proper lighting is crucial when working with intricate knots and patterns. Natural light is ideal, so, if possible, set up your crafting space near a window to take advantage of daylight. If natural light is not sufficient, consider investing in a good-quality desk lamp that provides bright, adjustable lighting. Position your lighting source in a way that minimizes shadows on your work surface, allowing you to see the details of your knots and patterns with ease. Adjustable lamps with flexible arms are great for directing light exactly where you need it. Additionally, consider the color temperature of the light – a cool white light can help you see colors accurately, while a warm light can create a cozy ambiance for your crafting sessions. By ensuring that your crafting area is well-lit, you'll not only improve the quality of your work but also make the creative process more comfortable and enjoyable. Good lighting is vital for precision in your macramé projects, so don't overlook this important aspect of your crafting setup.

Presently, you've acquired foundational knowledge about the essential tools required for a novice macramé crafter to thrive. Possessing the proper tools can significantly impact the quality of your finished projects. With a sturdy board, sharp scissors, support, measuring tape, comb and brush, crochet hook, cord dispenser, glue, needle and thread, cork pad and pins, S-hooks, storage box or basket for cords, lighting, and a rotary cutter, you are well-equipped to create beautiful pieces of macramé art. When picking out your first macramé kit, there are several factors to keep in mind to ensure a positive experience. Consider the complexity of the projects included in the kit and choose one that aligns with your skill level. Some kits are designed specifically for beginners, with detailed instructions and simple patterns to follow. Look for kits that provide a variety of cord colors and textures to allow for creativity in your designs. Additionally, consider the size of the finished projects and whether they align with your preferences. Some kits may focus on smaller decorative items, while others offer instructions for larger wall hangings or plant hangers.

Maximize your crafting experience by investing in high-quality tools that will endure for years to come. A trustworthy toolset will not only streamline your macramé process, but it will also empower you to branch out and try new techniques, feeling more confident with each project. Whether you're just starting out or a seasoned pro, having the right equipment will ignite your creativity and help you turn your ideas into reality. To get the most out of your macramé experience, set up a cozy workspace with excellent lighting and gather the essential tools you need to create. Don't be afraid to experiment with different patterns, colors, and cords – and remember to have fun! With your trusty tools by your side and a dash of imagination, you'll be well-equipped to tackle even the most ambitious projects.

2.2 Create the Perfect Macramé Workspace

Creating a harmonious and inspiring macramé space involves more than just setting up your workspace. Creating the perfect macramé space is all about setting yourself up for success. Whether you're a beginner or a seasoned pro, having a dedicated area for your crafting endeavors can make all the difference in your enjoyment and productivity. So, let's weave some magic into your space by crafting a cozy retreat that awakens your senses and sparks joy. In this section, we'll uncover insider secrets and innovative techniques for crafting a macramé oasis that revitalizes your mind, body, and soul.

First things first, let's talk about location. While you don't need a huge amount of space to enjoy macramé, it's important to choose a spot that offers ample room for you to work comfortably. **Indoor** spaces are ideal for those looking to create a cozy and intimate setting for their macramé practice. Any room with ample natural light, such as a sunny corner in your living room or a spacious home office, can be transformed into the perfect spot for your macramé projects.

Consider incorporating indoor plants, comfortable seating options, and good ventilation to enhance the ambiance of your indoor macramé space. Avoid high-traffic areas or places with limited natural light, as these can hinder your creative flow and overall enjoyment of the craft. Choosing the right **outdoor** location for your macramé projects is vital for connecting with nature and finding inspiration in the great outdoors. Whether it's a serene garden patio, a shaded spot under a tree, or a cozy backyard nook, any outdoor space can be transformed into a natural macramé setting. Macramé enthusiasts often find that being surrounded by nature enhances their creativity and overall well-being. Consider setting up your outdoor macramé space near a water feature or a garden full of blooming flowers to create a more tranquil and soothing environment for your craft. Macramé enthusiasts may find that being surrounded by nature enhances creativity and wellbeing. Enjoy the sounds of birds chirping or the rustling of leaves in the wind, which can bring a sense of peace and tranquility to your macramé practice. When choosing an outdoor space, be mindful of the weather and have a backup plan for inclement conditions so you can continue to enjoy your craft in any setting.

Of course, no macramé space is complete without a comfortable place to sit and work. A supportive **chair** with good back support is a must, especially if you plan to spend long hours knotting away. If you prefer to stand while you work, consider investing in a **standing desk** or a high table that allows you to work at a comfortable height. Another important consideration for your macramé space is the type of **work surface** you'll be using. A large, sturdy table or desk is ideal, as it will give you plenty of room to lay out your materials and work on larger projects. If you're short on space, a folding table or a lap desk can be a great alternative. Just be sure to choose a surface that is level and stable, to prevent your work from shifting or slipping as you knot. Additionally, position your work surface at a comfortable height to prevent hunching over your projects.

To enhance your macramé space and encourage creativity, consider incorporating **plants and decor** that inspire and uplift your mood. Adding plants to your workspace not only brings a touch of nature indoors but also helps in purifying the air and creating a refreshing atmosphere. Select plants that thrive indoors and are easy to care for, such as spider plants, pothos, or succulents. Choose decor pieces that resonate with your aesthetic and spark your imagination, whether it's a bohemian wall hanging, a calming vital oil diffuser, or a cozy throw blanket. Choose decor pieces such as inspirational quotes, artwork, or photos that resonate with your creative vibe and motivate you to keep crafting. By personalizing your space with elements that bring you joy, you can create a welcoming and inspiring environment for your macramé projects.

One of the joys of macramé is showcasing your beautiful creations. Consider incorporating a dedicated **display area** in your macramé space to exhibit your finished pieces and works-in-progress. A hanging wall shelf, a wooden dowel suspended from the ceiling, or a decorative branch hung on the wall can serve as stylish and functional display options. By showcasing your macramé works, you not only decorate your space but also draw inspiration from seeing your progress and creativity on display. To create an aesthetically pleasing display, consider mixing and matching different textures and sizes of macramé pieces. You can also add some greenery, such as hanging plants or dried flowers, to complement your creations and add a natural element to your space.

With macramé as the centerpiece of your space, consider incorporating wall arrangements and art that complement and highlight this intricate art form. Choose minimalist wall art or botanical prints to create a harmonious balance with the intricate knots and patterns of your macramé pieces. Additionally, consider mixing in metal accents or geometric shapes to add a modern touch to your bohemian space. The more you make your space a reflection of your personality and style, the more you'll enjoy spending time there.

The beauty of macramé is that it brings people together through a shared love of crafting. Creating a collaborative space in your macramé studio can help build a strong sense of community among fellow enthusiasts. Encourage others to share their work, ideas, and techniques, and consider hosting meetups or crafting circles to facilitate connections and inspire creativity. By fostering a supportive and inclusive environment, you can create a space where macramé lovers can learn from each other and grow together. **Collaborative Spaces** and Community Building are important components of a thriving macramé space. By inviting others to share their passion for the craft, you can create a vibrant and dynamic community that inspires creativity and fosters personal growth. Encourage collaboration, support, and inclusivity in your space, and watch as it blossoms into a hub of creativity and inspiration for all who enter.

Creating the perfect macramé space may take a bit of time and effort, but the payoff is well worth it. With a comfortable, well-organized, and inspiring workspace, you'll find yourself eager to throw yourself into your latest project and unravel all the wonderful possibilities that macramé has to offer. So go ahead and create a cozy niche for this charming craft – your creativity will thank you!

2.3 Ergonomic Matters: Creating a Comfortable Workspace

Macramé, with its intricate knots and rhythmic flow, can transport us to a state of creative euphoria. Yet, like any craft involving repetitive motions and focused attention, it's crucial to consider the ergonomics of our workspace. Ergonomics is all about designing a workspace that fits the user's needs, and in the case of macramé, that means creating a space that supports your body and encourages good posture. A well-designed workstation can help you avoid eye strain, back pain, and repetitive strain injuries, ensuring that you can continue crafting comfortably for years to come. When setting up your workstation, consider the following key elements:

Chair and Seating: Your chair is your throne when crafting, so choose wisely. Invest in a good-quality chair that provides lumbar support and allows you to sit with your feet flat on the floor. Ensure your thighs are parallel to the floor, and if your feet don't comfortably reach, consider using a footrest. Adjust your seat height so that your elbows are at a 90-degree angle when working, and ensure your forearms are supported. This will help reduce strain on your wrists and elbows. Also, resist the temptation to work in very soft, lounge-type chairs that might feel cozy at first but generally offer poor body support for crafting activities.

Table Height and Position: The ideal table height allows you to maintain a straight back and neutral wrist position when working without having to curve your spine into a question mark. If your table is too high or too low, consider using adjustable table legs or adding blocks under the legs to achieve the perfect height. Position your table so that you can sit squarely in front of it, avoiding twisting or reaching, which can cause back strain. One common mistake is using a work surface that's too small. This can lead to cramped workspaces and limit your movement. Make sure to have a spacious work surface that allows you to move freely and comfortably.

Lighting: Good lighting is crucial in macramé, especially when working with fine cords or intricate patterns. Natural light is ideal, so position your workstation near a window if possible. Ensure your workspace is well-lit from multiple angles to avoid shadows, which can cause eye strain. Consider using a combination of overhead lighting and task lighting, such as a desk lamp, to illuminate your work from different directions. Remove any excess glare from windows or mirrors in the area to prevent eyestrain. If you're working with smaller, detailed projects, consider using a magnifying lamp to reduce eye strain. Make sure to give your eyes regular breaks; follow the 20-20-20 rule – after every 20 minutes, take a 20-second break and look at something 20 feet away.

Storage and Organization: A cluttered workspace can impede your creativity and comfort. Design a storage system that keeps your cords, beads, and other supplies organized and within easy reach. Use drawers, shelves, or containers to categorize your items, ensuring that you don't have to stretch or lean frequently to access your tools. For bigger projects, you might want a tool belt or an apron with pockets.

Take Breaks: It's easy to get lost in the meditative process of knotting, but remember to give your body a rest. Set a timer to remind yourself to stretch every 30 minutes or so. Roll your shoulders, stretch your hands, walk around and maybe even do a little impromptu dance. It keeps the blood flowing and your creativity glowing. A few minutes of movement can prevent hours of stiffness. Don't forget to give your eyes a break too! Look away from your work and focus on something in the distance to reduce eye fatigue. One of the most common mistakes is ignoring discomfort. Listen to your body's whispers before they turn into shouts. Regular breaks are not just refreshing, but they are necessary to maintain your physical and mental well-being. Remember, it's better to take frequent short breaks than to push through discomfort and risk injury.

Now, let's address some **common issues and mistakes**. One common mistake many macramé enthusiasts make is neglecting their hand health. Repetitive motions and gripping can lead to hand fatigue and even conditions like carpal tunnel syndrome. To combat this, take regular breaks to stretch your fingers and wrists. Consider using ergonomic tools, such as cushioned grip scissors or pliers, to reduce hand strain. If you experience persistent pain or discomfort, don't hesitate to seek the advice of a healthcare professional. Also remember that working with tight cords can lead to hand and wrist strain, so make sure to loosen the cords before starting your work. You can also use a cord holder or a macramé board to keep the cords organized and at a comfortable tension.

In conclusion, prioritizing ergonomics in your macramé workstation is an investment in your long-term well-being and artistic growth. So, let's create beautiful macramé pieces while also unknotting yourself every now and then!

Chapter 3: Choosing The Perfect Macramé Cord

3.1 Mastering Macramé Terminology

If you're a novice in the fascinating domain of knotting and weaving, you might find yourself scratching your head when it comes to the terms "cord," "rope," "strand," "string," and "ply." The confusion around these terms is pretty common, and it's easy to see why. In everyday language, we often use these words interchangeably, without giving much thought to their specific meanings. But in the context of macramé, each term has a distinct definition and purpose, which can be a bit overwhelming for beginners. So, why the confusion? Well, it all comes down to the fact that these terms are often used inconsistently across different sources and communities. Some people might use "cord" and "rope" interchangeably, while others reserve "rope" for thicker materials. Similarly, "strand" and "string" might be used to refer to the same thing in one context, but have different meanings in another. And don't even get me started on "ply" - it's like the secret password of the macramé domain, and it requires a certain level of initiation to grasp its importance. But I'm here to assist you in unraveling the mystery and simplifying these terms in a manner that is straightforward and memorable. Now, let's examine the distinct characteristics of each macramé material.

First up, let's talk about the most common term you'll encounter: **cord**. In the sphere of macramé, a cord is like the dependable adjunct of your knotting pursuits. It's the go-to material for most projects, and it comes in a variety of sizes, colors, and textures. Cords are typically made from natural fibers like cotton, hemp, and jute, or synthetic materials like nylon and polyester. They're the all-purpose players of the macramé game, perfect for creating everything from delicate jewelry to bold wall hangings. The most common cord types, usually referred to simply as "cords," are the Braided and Single Twist varieties.

Next, we have **rope**. Now, here's where things can get a bit tricky. In general parlance, "rope" and "cord" are often used synonymously, but in macramé, rope usually refers to thicker, sturdier materials. Rope is made by twisting or braiding individual strands of fiber together. The way these strands are combined can vary, resulting in different types of rope like two-ply or three-ply, each offering a unique texture and strength. In macramé, both two-ply and three-ply ropes are frequently used, with each serving different aesthetic and functional purposes. Additionally, rope can be braided, which gives it a more uniform and durable structure. However, unlike string, when you attempt to brush out rope, the ends tend to become wavy rather than fluffy. Ropes are the big siblings of cords - they're chunkier, stronger, and ready to take on the heavy-duty projects. If you're looking to create a statement piece that can hold its own, like a large-scale wall hanging or a plant hanger that can support a hefty fern, rope is your best bet.

Moving on to strands and strings - these terms are often used interchangeably with cords, but there are some subtle differences. **Strand** typically refers to a single, thin length of fiber or material. In macramé, a strand can be one of the individual pieces that make up a thicker cord or rope. When multiple strands are twisted or braided together, they form a cord or rope. The term "strand" emphasizes the individual component that could be part of a larger whole. It's thin, delicate, and perfect for creating intricate, lacy designs. Think of it like a single strand of hair - it's fine, flexible, and adds a touch of elegance to your knotted creations. **String**, on the other hand, is often seen as a type of thin cord that's ready to use as is so it's a finished product on its own. It's generally thinner and less complex than what might be termed a "cord" or "rope." It's often made from materials like cotton, linen, or even silk, which offer a smooth, lustrous finish. String is perfect for creating smaller-scale items o for projects that require a more refined look like jewelry, bookmarks, or even delicate trim for other crafts. Its thin diameter allows for intricate knotting patterns and fine details that might get lost with thicker materials. It may not be as durable as cord or rope, so it's best suited for projects that won't see heavy wear and tear. One of the best things about cotton string is its ability to be brushed out, transforming into stunning tassels, feathery embellishments, and a myriad of other decorative elements. Typically, cords with a thickness of 1-2mm are referred to as "string". In contrast, any cord size (thickness) of 3mm or greater is defined as "cord".

Last but not least, let's talk about **plies**. Now, I know what you're thinking - "Plies? Isn't that a ballet move?" Well, in the field of macramé, plies are like the secret ingredient that determines the strength and texture of your cords. A ply refers to a single strand that's twisted together with others to create a thicker, stronger cord. Single-ply cords are made from one strand, while multi-ply cords are made from two or more strands twisted together. The number of plies affects the durability, texture, and overall look of your cord - single-ply cords are often softer and more pliable, while multi-ply cords offer more structure and support.

So, there you have it - the lowdown on cords, ropes, strands, strings, and plies. I hope this little crash course has helped clear up some of the confusion and given you a better understanding of the materials you'll be working with. But remember, the most important thing is to have fun and let your creativity shine through, no matter what you call your knotting medium. Don't get too caught up in the nuances of terminology - as you dig deeper into the area of macramé, you'll develop your own preferences and understanding of these terms.

3.2 The Best Macrame Cord Options for Your Creations

As a skilled crafter in macramé, you know that the choice of cord can greatly impact the final outcome of your project. With numerous options at your disposal, it's crucial to familiarize yourself with the unique traits, advantages, and intended uses of each material to guarantee a successful creation. From the earthy embrace of natural fibers to the sleek sophistication of synthetic strands, the perfect cord is ready to dance to the rhythm of your imagination. Get ready to be captivated by the boundless opportunities that macramé cords present. Let's immerse ourselves in the realm of macramé cord materials and uncover the vast potential!

3.2.1 Natural Fibers: The Eco-Friendly Choice

For those who prioritize sustainability and environmental consciousness, natural fibers are an excellent option. These fibers are biodegradable and have a significantly lower ecological footprint compared to their synthetic counterparts. Moreover, natural fibers lend a distinct, organic texture to your macramé projects, adding a unique charm and character to your creations. However, it's crucial to keep in mind that natural fibers may be more susceptible to shrinkage and stretching over time. This characteristic should be carefully considered when planning your macramé endeavors to ensure the longevity and quality of your finished product. Let's examine the prevailing natural materials commonly employed in macramé: cotton, hemp, jute, linen, silk and leather. Each of these fibers possesses its own unique properties and benefits, offering a diverse range of options for your macramé projects.

Cotton cord is a popular choice among macramé enthusiasts, and for good reason. This versatile and budget-friendly material is soft to the touch, making it a delight to work with. Cotton cords are available in a wide array of colors, ranging from natural and earthy tones to vibrant and bold hues, enabling you to create pieces that seamlessly complement your personal style and home décor. One of the primary advantages of using cotton cord is its user-friendly nature. The pliable and forgiving texture makes it an ideal option for beginners who are still honing their knotting skills. Moreover, cotton's high absorbency allows for the creation of functional items such as plant hangers, kitchen towels, and even bath mats. When choosing cotton cords for your macramé projects, it is essential to select high-quality, long-staple cotton that is smooth and free from defects. This attention to detail will guarantee that your knots are uniform and your finished piece exudes a polished, professional appearance. With its vast color selection, ease of use, and versatility, cotton cord is an excellent material for crafting stunning and practical macramé creations.

For those who prioritize sustainability and durability, **hemp cord** is a fantastic choice. Made from the fibers of the hemp plant, a fast-growing, renewable resource that requires minimal pesticides and fertilizers to cultivate, hemp is an excellent option for environmentally conscious individuals looking to minimize their impact on the planet. Hemp cords have a slightly rougher texture compared to cotton, adding a rustic and natural look to your macramé creations. Their incredible strength makes them ideal for creating items that require significant weight-bearing, such as hammocks, chair swings, and large wall hangings. Hemp's natural resistance to mold, mildew, and UV rays ensures that your macramé pieces will remain beautiful for years to come, even when exposed to the elements. When working with hemp cords, keep in mind that they may be a bit stiffer than other natural fibers, requiring more effort to manipulate initially. However, as you work with them, the cords will soften over time, becoming more pliable and comfortable to handle.

One final consideration when using hemp cord is its slight natural odor, which will gradually fade away, leaving you with a pleasant reminder of its origin and connection to the environment.

Jute cord has become increasingly popular among macramé enthusiasts, especially those who adore a bohemian or rustic aesthetic. Derived from the outer stem and skin of the jute plant, this cord boasts a distinctive, slightly coarse texture that infuses your projects with depth and character. Renowned for their robustness and longevity, jute cords are perfect for larger-scale projects or items subjected to frequent use, such as table runners or hanging chairs. Moreover, their biodegradable and compostable nature makes them an environmentally conscious choice for those seeking to minimize their ecological impact. The natural golden hue of jute effortlessly complements a wide array of color palettes and design styles, ranging from beachy and coastal to warm and earthy. When working with jute cord, it's essential to keep in mind that it may be slightly less flexible compared to cotton or hemp. Take your time when crafting knots and be gentle to prevent excessive strain on the fibers. With a bit of patience, you'll be able to create breathtaking, texture-rich pieces that showcase the unparalleled beauty of jute, captivating the eye and elevating your macramé creations to new heights.

Linen, a sumptuous natural fiber derived from the flax plant, has been cherished for centuries in various applications, ranging from garments to interior décor. Its strength, longevity, and elegant appearance make it a highly sought-after material. Linen cords possess a slightly coarse, organic texture that lends a rustic allure to any creation. Moreover, their exceptional absorbency and quick-drying properties render them an ideal choice for items that may encounter water, such as bath mats or kitchen towels. One of the remarkable features of linen is its inherent antibacterial qualities, which enable it to resist the growth of mold and mildew, making it a hygienic option for products intended for use in humid environments. Additionally, linen cords exhibit excellent shape retention, making them perfect for projects that demand substantial structure, such as wall hangings or plant hangers. When choosing linen cords for your macramé endeavors, it is essential to opt for premium, tightly-woven cords with a uniform thickness throughout. Although linen may be slightly more costly compared to other natural fibers, its exquisite beauty and unparalleled durability make it a valuable investment for exceptional projects.

If you're looking to add a touch of luxury to your macramé projects, consider using **silk cords**. Silk, a natural protein fiber produced by silkworms, is renowned for its exquisite sheen, softness, and strength. Although not as commonly used in macramé as other natural fibers, silk can elevate your projects with a sense of elegance and sophistication. Silk cords possess a smooth, lustrous texture that beautifully catches the light, creating a glamorous effect. Despite their delicate appearance, these cords are incredibly strong and durable, making them an excellent choice for intricate designs that require extensive knotting and manipulation. As a naturally hypoallergenic and dust mite-resistant material, silk is perfect for those with allergies or sensitivities. When working with silk cords, it's essential to handle them with care to prevent fraying, as they may be more delicate than other natural fibers.

Additionally, silk cords can be slightly slippery, requiring extra patience and practice to achieve even knots. However, the stunning results are well worth the effort. Silk macramé projects create beautiful decorative accents, such as wall hangings, table runners, or even unique jewelry pieces. The incorporation of silk elevates the overall aesthetic of these projects, adding a touch of luxury and refinement to any space. While working with silk may require a bit more finesse, the end results are sure to impress and add a touch of luxury to any space.

When selecting natural fibers for your macramé projects, consider the specific characteristics and benefits of each material and how they align with your project goals and personal preferences. Cotton is a versatile, beginner-friendly option that offers endless color possibilities, while hemp is a strong, eco-friendly choice that adds rustic charm to your pieces. Jute is an affordable, biodegradable option with an earthy, bohemian vibe, while linen offers a luxurious, sophisticated touch with its smooth texture and natural antibacterial properties. Silk adds a touch of glamour and elegance to your projects with its lustrous sheen and delicate strength. No matter which natural fiber you choose, you can feel good about using a sustainable, biodegradable material that showcases the beauty and versatility of nature in your macramé creations.

3.2.2 Synthetic Options

If you're looking for a more budget-friendly and durable option, synthetic cords may be the way to go. While natural fibers like cotton and hemp have their own unique charm, synthetic cords offer a range of benefits that make them a popular choice among crafters. In this subchapter, we'll enter into a thorough examination of synthetic macramé cords, specifically concentrating on nylon, polyester, and polypropylene options.

Nylon is a synthetic fiber that has earned its place as a top choice for macramé enthusiasts due to its impressive strength, durability, and smooth texture. When you work with nylon cord, you can expect your macramé projects to have a sleek, polished appearance that showcases the intricate knots and patterns you've created. One of the most significant advantages of nylon cord is its resistance to stretching and shrinking, ensuring that your macramé pieces maintain their shape and structure over time, even with regular use. Nylon cord is incredibly versatile, making it suitable for a wide range of macramé applications. Whether you're crafting indoor décor items like wall hangings and plant hangers or creating outdoor accessories such as lawn chairs or hammocks, nylon cord can withstand exposure to various elements, including sun, rain, and humidity, without deteriorating or losing its strength. This durability makes it an excellent investment for crafters who want their macramé projects to last for years to come. Another appealing aspect of nylon cord is the extensive color selection available. From classic neutrals to vibrant, eye-catching hues, you can find nylon cord in virtually any color you desire, allowing you to create macramé pieces that perfectly complement your personal style or home décor. Additionally, nylon cord is relatively affordable compared to some natural fibers, making it a feasible choice for newcomers who are just starting their initiation into the field of macramé without breaking the bank.

Polyester cord has become increasingly popular among macramé enthusiasts, and for good reason. This synthetic fiber is known for its incredible softness and suppleness, making it a pleasure to work with, even for extended periods. The smooth, pliable texture of polyester cord is gentle on the hands, reducing the risk of fatigue or discomfort as you create your intricate macramé designs. This is particularly important for beginners who are still developing their knotting techniques and building up hand strength. One of the most appealing characteristics of polyester cord is its subtle sheen, which adds a touch of elegance and sophistication to your finished macramé pieces. This lustrous quality catches the light beautifully, highlighting the intricacy of your knots and patterns, and elevating the overall appearance of your creations. Whether you're crafting a delicate wall hanging or a statement-making plant hanger, the gentle shimmer of polyester cord is sure to make your projects stand out. Polyester cord is also highly resistant to fraying, a common issue that can detract from the polished look of your macramé pieces. With polyester, you can create complex designs with confidence, knowing that your cord will maintain its integrity and structure, even with frequent handling or use. This durability makes polyester cord an excellent choice for crafting functional items like macramé bags, placemats, or coasters, which may be subject to regular wear and tear. Like nylon cord, polyester is available in a wide spectrum of colors, from soft pastels to rich, vibrant hues. This versatility allows you to create macramé projects that perfectly match your personal aesthetic or complement your existing home décor. Whether you prefer a bohemian, minimalist, or contemporary style, you can find polyester cord in colors to suit your aesthetic preferences. It's worth noting that polyester cord may have slightly more stretch than nylon, which is important to keep in mind when planning your macramé projects. This flexibility can be advantageous in certain situations, such as when creating pieces that require a bit of give or drape, like wall hangings or curtains. However, for projects that demand a firmer, more structured hold, such as plant hangers or jewelry, you may want to consider using a cord with less stretch, like nylon or polypropylene. Overall, polyester cord is an excellent choice for macramé enthusiasts of all skill levels, offering a winning combination of softness, suppleness, and durability.

Polypropylene cord has recently gained significant popularity in the macramé community, thanks to its unique set of properties that make it an ideal choice for a variety of projects. One of the most notable characteristics of polypropylene cord is its incredibly lightweight nature. This makes it perfect for crafting large-scale macramé pieces, such as wall hangings, room dividers, or even outdoor installations, without adding excessive weight that could compromise the integrity of the structure or make it difficult to hang or display. Another major advantage of polypropylene cord is its waterproof properties. Unlike natural fibers like cotton or hemp, which can absorb moisture and become prone to mildew or deterioration, polypropylene cord is completely resistant to water. This makes it an excellent choice for crafting macramé pieces that will be exposed to humid environments, such as bathroom or kitchen décor, outdoor plant hangers, or even pool or beach accessories. You can confidently use polypropylene cord in these settings, knowing that it will maintain its strength, shape, and appearance, even when subjected to moisture. In addition to being waterproof, polypropylene cord is also highly resistant to UV rays. This means that it won't fade, discolor, or degrade when exposed to direct sunlight, making it the perfect material for outdoor macramé projects. Whether you're creating a stunning macramé hammock for your backyard oasis, a set of decorative plant hangers for your patio, or even a unique outdoor art installation, polypropylene cord will withstand the elements beautifully, ensuring that your creations remain vibrant and sturdy for years to come. Polypropylene cord has a matte finish, which offers a more understated and natural look compared to the slight sheen of polyester or the high gloss of some nylon cords. This subtle texture can add a sense of depth and dimension to your macramé pieces, creating a beautifully organic and tactile aesthetic. While the color selection for polypropylene cord may be more limited compared to other synthetic options, you can still find a range of versatile hues that will work well for a variety of macramé applications. When working with polypropylene cord, it's important to keep in mind that it may have a slightly stiffer texture compared to the suppleness of polyester or the smoothness of nylon. This can make it a bit more challenging to work with, especially for intricate designs or complex knots. However, as you become more comfortable with the material and develop your macramé skills, you'll find that polypropylene cord's unique properties make it an invaluable addition to your crafting toolkit.

In summary, synthetic macramé cords, such as nylon, polyester, and polypropylene, offer a wealth of options for crafters looking to create stunning, durable, and versatile projects. Each type of cord has its own unique set of characteristics and benefits, making it easy to find the perfect material to suit your specific needs and creative vision. Nylon cord is a strong, smooth, and versatile choice that works well for both indoor and outdoor projects, while polyester cord is soft, supple, and easy to work with, making it ideal for creating intricate designs and functional items. Polypropylene cord, on the other hand, is lightweight, waterproof, and UV-resistant, making it the go-to choice for outdoor macramé pieces and large-scale installations. By understanding the unique characteristics of each type of cord and choosing the right one for your project, you'll be well on your way to creating stunning macramé pieces that will stand the test of time.

3.2.3 Blended Cords: The Best of Both Worlds

While natural fibers and synthetic options each have their own unique benefits, there's a third category that deserves equal attention: **blended cords**. Blended macramé cords are created by combining natural and synthetic fibers in varying proportions, resulting in a material that showcases the strengths of both components. These hybrid cords offer a unique balance of properties, allowing crafters to enjoy the beauty and eco-friendliness of natural fibers while benefiting from the durability and ease of care provided by synthetic materials. Some common blends include cotton-polyester, hemp-nylon, and linen-acrylic, each with its own distinct characteristics and advantages.

One of the most popular blended cord options is the **cotton-polyester** blend. This combination brings together the softness and breathability of cotton with the strength and resilience of polyester. Cotton-polyester blends are ideal for crafting macramé projects that require a supple, comfortable feel, such as clothing accessories, cushion covers, or even baby items. The polyester content helps to minimize shrinkage and enhance the cord's resistance to wear and tear, making these blends a practical choice for items that will be subject to regular use or washing. When working with cotton-polyester blends, you'll find that they have a slightly fuzzy texture, which can add a cozy, tactile element to your macramé designs. These blends are available in a wide range of colors, from natural, earthy tones to vibrant, eye-catching hues, allowing you to create pieces that perfectly match your aesthetic preferences. As a beginner, starting with a medium-weight cotton-polyester blend can be a great way to familiarize yourself with the material and practice your knotting techniques.

For crafters who prioritize eco-friendliness and durability, **hemp-nylon** blends offer an attractive solution. Hemp, a natural fiber known for its strength and sustainability, is combined with nylon, a synthetic material that boasts excellent resilience and resistance to wear. This combination results in a cord that is both environmentally conscious and long-lasting, perfect for crafting macramé projects that will stand the test of time. Hemp-nylon blends have a slightly rougher texture compared to cotton-polyester blends, which can add an interesting visual and tactile dimension to your macramé designs. These blends work particularly well for outdoor projects, such as plant hangers, wall hangings, or even furniture accents, as they can withstand exposure to the elements without deteriorating. The nylon content also helps to reduce stretching and maintain the shape of your macramé pieces over time.

For a touch of sophistication and easy maintenance, ponder taking a closer look at **linen-acrylic** blends. Linen, a natural fiber derived from flax plants, is known for its crisp, elegant appearance and excellent drape. When combined with acrylic, a synthetic fiber that offers softness, lightness, and resistance to wrinkles, the resulting blend is a versatile and low-maintenance option for your macramé projects. Linen-acrylic blends have a smooth, sleek texture that lends itself well to creating intricate, detailed macramé designs. These blends are perfect for crafting home décor items, such as table runners, placemats, or decorative wall hangings, as they have a refined, upscale look that can elevate any space. The acrylic content makes these blends easy to care for, as they can be machine washed and dried without losing their shape or texture.

To recap, blended macramé cords offer crafters an exciting opportunity to combine the best qualities of natural and synthetic fibers, resulting in materials that are both beautiful and practical. By combining different fibers in varying proportions, you can create custom blends that showcase the specific qualities you desire in your macramé projects. Whether you're looking for a particular color combination, texture, or weight, experimenting with your own blends allows you to tailor your cords to your exact preferences. When blending your own cords, it's essential to consider the compatibility of the fibers you're using. Some fibers may have different shrinkage rates or care requirements, which can affect the longevity and appearance of your finished projects. It's also important to test your custom blends before committing to a large-scale project, ensuring that the resulting cord meets your expectations in terms of strength, texture, and overall performance. Whether you opt for a cotton-polyester blend for its softness and strength, a hemp-nylon blend for its eco-friendliness and durability, or a linen-acrylic blend for its elegance and ease of care, these hybrid cords unlock a vast array of innovative opportunities for your macramé projects.

3.2.4 Specialty Cords: Adding a Touch of Uniqueness

In the constantly shifting landscape of macramé, artisans are perpetually on the hunt for fresh and thrilling supplies to enhance their creations and stretch the limits of innovation. While natural fibers, synthetic options, and blended cords offer a wide range of possibilities, there's another category that calls for a closer inspection: **specialty cords**. They are made from unique materials or have special features that set them apart from traditional macramé cords. These unique and innovative materials open up a whole new realm of textures, colors, and effects, allowing you to create macramé pieces that truly stand out from the crowd. Let's slide into the fascinating arena of specialty cords, uncovering their distinct characteristics, creative applications, and the endless opportunities they provide for your macramé pursuits.

Beaded cords represent a fascinating niche within the broader spectrum of macramé specialty cords, offering a unique blend of texture, visual appeal, and personalization to the craft. Unlike traditional macramé cords, which are uniform in texture and color, beaded cords introduce an element of decorative flair through the incorporation of beads directly onto the cord before the knotting process begins. This integration of beads allows for an array of design possibilities, enabling crafters to infuse their projects with varying degrees of color, shine, and dimensionality. The beads themselves can be of diverse materials, including glass, wood, metal, or plastic, each adding its own character and weight to the piece. The choice of bead material and design directly influences the overall aesthetic and functional outcome of the project, whether it be a delicate piece of jewelry, an ornate wall hanging, or a chic plant hanger. The process of working with beaded cords requires a thoughtful approach to design and planning, as the placement of beads must be considered in relation to the macramé knots and patterns. This meticulous integration not only enhances the tactile experience of creating macramé but also elevates the finished product to a work of art, characterized by depth and intricacy.

If you're looking to infuse your macramé projects with a bit of sparkle and shine, **metallic cords** are the perfect choice. These eye-catching cords feature a lustrous, shimmery finish that catches the light beautifully, adding a touch of glamour and sophistication to your designs. Metallic cords are available in a range of colors, from classic gold and silver to trendy rose gold and copper, allowing you to create macramé pieces that exude luxury and elegance. One of the most appealing aspects of metallic cords is their versatility. They can be used on their own to create stunning statement pieces, such as wall hangings, jewelry, or even fashion accessories. Alternatively, you can incorporate metallic cords alongside other materials, like natural fibers or synthetic options, to add a pop of shimmer and visual interest to your macramé designs. When working with metallic cords, keep in mind that they may have a slightly stiffer texture compared to traditional cords, so it's essential to practice your knotting techniques and adjust your tension accordingly.

Waxed cords have emerged as a game-changer in the field of macramé, offering crafters a unique and versatile material that combines both style and functionality. These innovative cords are created by applying a thin layer of wax to various fibers, such as cotton or polyester, resulting in a material that boasts both aesthetic appeal and enhanced functionality. The wax coating gives these cords a distinct, lustrous appearance, with a smooth, almost glossy surface that catches the light beautifully. This subtle sheen can elevate the overall look of your macramé projects, adding a touch of elegance and sophistication to even the most basic knots and patterns. In addition to their visual appeal, waxed cords offer several practical benefits that make them a go-to choice for many macramé enthusiasts. The wax coating acts as a protective barrier, shielding the underlying fibers from dirt, dust, and moisture, thereby increasing the durability and longevity of your creations. This makes waxed cords particularly well-suited for projects that will be exposed to the elements or subjected to frequent use, such as outdoor wall hangings, plant hangers, or even jewelry and accessories. Another significant advantage of waxed cords is their resistance to fraying and tangling, two common issues that can arise when working with uncoated cords. The smooth, cohesive surface created by the wax coating helps to prevent individual fibers from splitting or unraveling, allowing you to create clean, precise knots and patterns without the frustration of constantly dealing with frayed ends. This feature is especially beneficial when working on intricate or delicate designs that require frequent manipulation of the cords. Waxed cords also offer a unique tactile experience, with a smooth, almost silky feel that can be particularly enjoyable when working on complex knots and patterns. The slick surface helps to minimize friction between cords, making it easier to tighten and adjust your knots as you work, ultimately leading to a more consistent and professional-looking result. This ease of use, combined with the cords' durability and fraying resistance, makes waxed cords an excellent choice for both beginners and experienced macramé crafters alike.

When working with waxed cords, it's essential to keep a few tips in mind to ensure the best results. Due to the slick nature of the wax coating, you may need to apply slightly more tension when tightening your knots to achieve a secure hold. If you find that your knots are slipping or not holding as desired, try gently rubbing the cords between your fingers to warm up the wax and create a tacky surface that improves grip. Always use sharp, clean scissors when cutting waxed cords to ensure a neat, precise cut and minimize fraying. Lastly, to maintain the longevity and appearance of your waxed cord projects, store them in a cool, dry place away from direct sunlight or extreme temperatures, which can degrade the wax coating over time.

For a bold and unexpected twist on traditional macramé, consider stepping into the territory of **leather cords**. These specialty cords bring a sense of rustic charm and modern edge to your projects, creating a striking contrast against the soft, fluid nature of classic macramé designs. They are available in various thicknesses, colors, and finishes, from sleek and polished to distressed and vintage-inspired, allowing you to create pieces that perfectly match your personal style. These cords are particularly well-suited for crafting macramé jewelry, such as bracelets, necklaces, and earrings. The durability and strength of leather make these pieces long-lasting and able to withstand daily wear and tear. You can also incorporate leather cords into larger macramé projects, like wall hangings or plant hangers, to add a unique textural element and a touch of bohemian flair. When working with leather cords, it's important to use sharp scissors or a leather cutter to ensure clean, precise cuts, and to condition the leather regularly to maintain its suppleness and prevent cracking.

For a softer, more fluid approach to macramé, **ribbon cords** offer an elegant and graceful option. These flat, wide cords are typically made from materials like satin, silk, or velvet, and they create a distinctly different look and feel compared to traditional twisted or braided cords. Ribbon cords are perfect for crafting macramé projects that require a delicate, flowing appearance, such as wall hangings, curtain ties, or even bridal accessories. One of the key advantages of working with ribbon cords is their ability to create intricate, detailed knots and patterns. The flat surface of the ribbon allows for clean, crisp lines and a more graphic, modern aesthetic. Ribbon cords are available in a wide array of colors and patterns, from soft pastels to bold, vibrant prints, enabling you to create macramé pieces that are truly one-of-a-kind. When using ribbon cords, it's crucial to take care when tightening your knots, as the material may be more prone to fraying or snagging compared to traditional cords.

For the macramé enthusiast who loves to think outside the box, **novelty cords** offer an endless array of creative possibilities. These specialty cords come in a variety of unconventional materials, textures, and shapes, allowing you to push the boundaries of traditional macramé and create truly unique, eye-catching pieces. Some examples of novelty cords include:

1. Jute cords with metallic flecks

2. Cords made from recycled materials, like plastic or fabric scraps

3. Glow-in-the-dark cords for a magical, luminescent effect

4. Cords with embedded beads or sequins for added texture and sparkle

5. Felted wool cords for a cozy, rustic feel

When working with novelty cords, let your imagination run wild and don't be afraid to experiment with different combinations and techniques. These specialty materials can be used on their own or combined with traditional cords to create one-of-a-kind macramé masterpieces that showcase your individual style and creativity.

As with any macramé material, *proper care and maintenance* are essential to ensure the longevity and beauty of your specialty cord projects. Each type of cord may have specific care requirements, depending on its material composition and texture. For example, metallic cords may tarnish over time and require gentle polishing, while leather cords may need regular conditioning to prevent drying and cracking. By taking the time to properly care for your specialty cords, you'll ensure that your macramé creations remain stunning and vibrant for years to come.

From the glamorous shimmer of metallic cords to the rustic charm of leather, the soft drape of ribbon cords to the endless possibilities of novelty materials, not to mention the unique and customizable allure of beaded cords, these specialty options unlock a universe of inspiration and innovation. Don't be afraid to push the boundaries of traditional macramé, embrace experimentation and let your creativity shine. By incorporating these extraordinary materials into your designs, you'll create macramé pieces that not only showcase your skills and imagination but also convey a narrative of your distinctive artistic path. Each cord type brings its own distinct vibe and potential, enabling you to craft not just items, but experiences, and connections woven through the threads of your creativity.

3.2.5 Recycled Yarns: Creative Upcycling

For those who love to get creative with their macramé projects, **recycled yarns** offer an opportunity to upcycle old materials and give them new life. You can use recycled t-shirt yarn, also known as "tarn," which is made by cutting old t-shirts into long, continuous strips. This eco-friendly option is soft, stretchy, and adds a unique texture to your macramé creations. Other recycled yarn options include repurposed fabric strips, plastic bags, or even old bedsheets. By repurposing these materials, recycled yarns help to divert waste from landfills, conserve natural resources, and minimize the carbon footprint associated with traditional yarn production.

The process of creating recycled yarns varies depending on the specific material being used. For example, **recycled plastic yarns** are typically made by breaking down plastic bottles into small flakes, melting them, and then extruding the molten plastic into fine, continuous filaments. These filaments are then spun into yarns, ready to be used in a wide range of applications, including macramé. Similarly, **recycled cotton yarns** are often made from post-consumer clothing or textile waste, which is sorted by color, shredded, and then re-spun into new yarns.

Beyond their environmental benefits, recycled yarns offer a range of advantages for macramé enthusiasts. One of the most appealing aspects of these cords is their unique texture and appearance. Recycled yarns often have a slightly irregular, rustic look that adds character and depth to your macramé projects. This distinctive aesthetic can help your pieces stand out and tell a story of sustainability and creativity. Another benefit of recycled yarns is their durability. Many recycled materials, such as plastic or denim, are inherently strong and resilient, making them ideal for crafting long-lasting macramé projects. These cords can withstand the wear and tear of daily use, ensuring that your creations remain beautiful and functional for years to come. Recycled yarns also offer a wide range of colors and textures to choose from. As these cords are made from repurposed materials, they often showcase a mix of hues and shades that reflect their original sources. This variety allows you to create visually interesting, one-of-a-kind macramé pieces that are truly reflective of your personal style and creativity. The possibilities for incorporating recycled yarns into your macramé projects are endless. These versatile cords can be used in a wide range of applications, from wall hangings and plant hangers to jewelry and accessories. One of the joys of macramé is the freedom to experiment and get creative with your cord choices. For example, you might combine a sturdy hemp cord for the main structure of a wall hanging with soft cotton cords for intricate, decorative knots. Or, you could incorporate a pop of luxurious leather cord into a primarily jute piece for an unexpected and eye-catching detail. By playing with different cord combinations, you'll expand your skills and unlock new possibilities for creating stunning, textural works of art that will be cherished for years to come.

3.3 Cord Foundations: Key Characteristics Unveiled

You know that feeling when you're excited to begin your next macramé project, but suddenly realize you're stuck on which cord to choose? Don't worry it's a common dilemma. Choosing the right macramé cord is just as crucial as picking out the perfect cake recipe for a celebration. You want to make sure you have all the right ingredients in the correct proportions to make your cake a hit. Similarly, the right cord is essential for your project to come together perfectly. So, let's break down everything you need to know about the fundamentals of macramé cord basics. By the end of this subchapter, you'll be a cord expert, ready to tackle any macramé project that comes your way.

3.3.1 Size and Thickness

In the matter of understanding macramé cord characteristics, familiarizing yourself with measurements such as millimeters, ply, and weight is imperative. **Millimeters** refer to the diameter of the cord and are commonly used to indicate cord thickness. **Ply** signifies the number of strands twisted together to create the cord, with a higher ply count resulting in a thicker cord. Additionally, cord **weight** is measured in grams per meter or ounces per yard, giving you an idea of the density and thickness of the cord.

Thinner cords, like the **micro cord** (less than 1mm) and 2mm cord, are perfect for creating delicate, intricate designs. These sizes are ideal for jewelry pieces, such as bracelets and necklaces, or for adding fine detailing to larger projects. As you move up in size, you'll find that **3mm and 4mm cords** are the sweet spot for many macramé lovers. These sizes offer a great balance between thickness and flexibility, making them suitable for a wide range of projects, from wall hangings and plant hangers to decorative items of various sizes. For those looking to make a bold statement, **5mm and 6mm** cords are the way to go. These thicker cords add substantial texture and visual interest to your pieces, making them perfect for larger wall hangings, statement plant hangers, and more robust items that demand attention. And let's not forget about the big guns – **8mm cords and above**! These chunky cords are reserved for heavy-duty projects that require serious strength and durability. Think macramé furniture (like chairs or hammocks), outdoor projects, and rugs that can withstand some serious foot traffic.

Cord Size	Use	Characteristic
Micro Cord (<2mm)	Ideal for delicate jewelry, small ornaments, and intricate detailing.	Offers fine detail work, not suitable for structural projects.
Thin Cord (2mm to 3mm)	Great for small-scale projects like bracelets, keychains, and detailed sections of larger pieces.	More detail-oriented than thicker cords but with increased strength.
Medium Cord (4mm to 5mm)	The most versatile size, suitable for a wide range of projects including wall hangings, plant hangers, and medium-sized decorative items.	Balances ease of use with substantial texture and structural integrity.
Thick Cord (6mm to 8mm)	Ideal for larger projects that require more structure, such as rugs, hammocks, and large wall art.	Provides a chunky, textured appearance and robust strength.
Extra Thick Cord (>8mm)	Used for very large and heavy-duty projects, including outdoor Macramé pieces, furniture, and bold decorative items.	Creates a very pronounced texture and is the most durable for heavy-weight applications.

Keep in mind that the thickness of the cord will also impact the size and tightness of your knots, so it's important to choose a cord that complements your design vision. So, the next time you begin on a macramé project, don't overlook the importance of choosing the right cord size. Take the time to assess your needs, make informed decisions, and enjoy the process of creating something beautiful with the perfect cord size. Your finished macramé piece will thank you for the attention to detail and careful consideration you put into selecting the right macramé cord size.

3.3.2 Strength and Twist

At the time to choose the best cord for your project, the cord structure is another important differentiator factor that can make all the difference on the overall look. Some cord structures may offer more flexibility, making them ideal for intricate knot work, while others may be more rigid and better suited for supporting heavier pieces. By considering the intended use of your macramé creation, you can choose a cord structure that will enhance the functionality and aesthetics of your project. Just like how we need strong muscles to power through our day, macramé cords need strength to withstand the tension and manipulation of knotting. The stronger the cord, the more durable your finished piece will be. Natural fibers like hemp and synthetic options like nylon are the stalwarts of the cord universe - they can handle even the most demanding projects without breaking a sweat. But strength isn't everything - the twist of your cord also plays a crucial role. The twist of a cord describes how tightly or loosely the fibers are spun together. A tighter twist results in a firmer, less stretchy cord that holds its shape like a boss. If you're working on a project that needs structure and definition, like a sleek wall hanging or a modern plant hanger, tightly twisted cords are your best friend. On the flip side, looser twists offer more flexibility and drape, allowing you to create flowing, bohemian-inspired pieces that are as free-spirited as you are. The tightness of the twist also affects the cord's behavior - a tighter twist results in a firmer, less stretchy cord, while a looser twist offers more flexibility and drape.

You will encounter three main types of cord structures: single stranded, twisted and braided. First up, we have the **single strand cord**. This type of cord is composed of multiple individual fibers twisted together in a single direction, forming a cohesive and unified cord. Known for its soft appearance, the single strand cord offers a delicate touch to any project. When brushed out, it yields a neat, straight fringe, making it an ideal choice for those dreamy wall hangings or any piece where a clean, flowing fringe is desired. Its versatility and ease of handling make it a favorite among macramé artists.

Next, let's talk about the **twisted cord** (multiple-ply cord). It consists of either two, three or 4 strands, twisted together to form a single cord or rope-like look. A *three ply cord*, as the name suggests, includes three such groups. This structure gives the cord a bit more rigidity compared to the single strand. It is less likely to unravel and is perfect for projects that require more structure, like plant hangers and wall hangings. This characteristic adds depth and interest to your pieces, providing a different aesthetic than the single strand cord.

Lastly, we come to the **braided cord.** It is made up of multiple strands woven together, resulting in a smooth and uniform appearance. This type of cord is known for its strength and durability, making it a popular choice for macramé projects that require sturdiness. Attempting to fray the ends of a braided cord could result in damaged fibers rather than a fluffy fringe. If your macramé creation doesn't involve fringes or tassels, a braided cord could be your go-to choice.

Twist Type	Pros	Cons	Impact on Beginners	Ideas for Beginners
Single Ply Cord	Very flexible, softer texture, ideal for delicate projects.	Less strength, more prone to fraying.	Great for practicing basic knots and creating delicate projects; requires careful handling to avoid fraying.	Delicate jewelry, small wall hangings, bookmarks.
2-Ply Cord	Good balance between strength and flexibility, more texture.	May twist under tension, limited strength for heavy projects.	Suitable for a wider range of projects; learning to manage twisting can be valuable.	Keychains, simple plant hangers, friendship bracelets.
3-Ply Cord	Stronger and more durable, suitable for a variety of projects, less likely to fray.	Less flexible, bulkier texture may not suit delicate designs.	Good for exploring beyond delicate projects; forgiving material for learners.	Medium wall hangings, plant hangers, market bags.
Braided Cord	Very strong, resistant to fraying, smooth texture.	Less flexible, can be more expensive.	Excellent for durable projects; reduced flexibility can be a limitation.	Durable plant hangers, coasters, sturdy keychains.

Regardless of category or ply, cords can feature an *S-Twist* or a *Z-Twist*. These terms refer to the direction in which the fibers or strands of a cord are twisted together, and they can apply to cords of varying ply counts, including single-ply (single twist), multi-ply, and even braided cords in some contexts. These terms are not exclusive to multi-ply cords but are used to describe the twist direction of any cord, whether it consists of a single strand or multiple strands twisted together. In the **S-Twist** type, fibers are twisted in a clockwise manner, creating a shape that resembles the middle section of the letter "S". Conversely, the **Z-Twist** type involves twisting fibers counterclockwise, resulting in a form that mimics the central part of the letter "Z". These twists are all the rage because they cater to a wide range of project needs, from durability and strength to achieving that perfect texture or making your crafting experience a breeze. Each twist has its own *special something*, making certain types better suited for specific projects. The decision on which twist to choose ultimately boils down to personal preference, the unique demands of your project, and how the cord behaves when you're working your magic with those knots. So, my advice? Get to know these common twists like the back of your hand. Once you understand what makes each one special, you'll be able to choose the best cord for your Macramé creations every single time. And trust me, when you've got the right cord in your hands, you'll be able to create something that's not just beautiful, but functional too.

3.3.3 Unlocking Cord Secrets: Beyond Basic Qualities

Moving forward with our examination of the foundational characteristics of macramé cord materials, size, thickness, strength and twist, it's important to consider also the intricate aspects that define their quality and suitability for various projects. From the texture and stiffness that define your work's personality to the strength and durability that ensure its longevity, each characteristic plays a pivotal role. We'll examine how consistency, smoothness, flexibility, and softness impact your crafting experience, alongside the importance of color fastness, sustainable and eco-friendly options, versatility and compatibility with various projects, and the ever-critical balance between price and value.

Texture and Stiffness

The texture and stiffness of your macramé cords can greatly impact the look and feel of your finished piece. Some cords, like cotton, have a soft and slightly fuzzy texture, while others, such as hemp or jute, have a rougher, more rustic feel. The stiffness of the cord also varies depending on the material and construction. Stiffer cords can create more defined knots and patterns, while softer cords may result in a more relaxed and flowing design. Consider the desired aesthetic of your project when choosing cords based on texture and stiffness.

Strength and Durability

First and foremost, you want your macramé cords to be strong and durable. After all, you're putting a lot of time and effort into your creations, and you want them to last! Look for cords that can withstand the tension and manipulation of knotting without breaking or fraying. Natural fibers like cotton, hemp, and linen are known for their strength and durability, making them excellent choices for macramé. Synthetic fibers like nylon and polyester are also incredibly strong and can be a good option for outdoor projects or items that will see a lot of wear and tear. When selecting cords, consider the intended use and longevity of your project to choose materials that will stand the test of time.

Consistency and Smoothness

The consistency and smoothness of your cords can make a big difference in the overall look and feel of your macramé pieces. Ideally, you want cords that have a consistent thickness throughout, without any thin or thick spots that could affect the appearance of your knots. Smoothness is also key - cords with a smooth, even texture will be easier to work with and will create cleaner, more polished-looking knots. When purchasing macramé cords, examine them closely to ensure that they are uniform in size and have a smooth, even surface throughout the length of the cord.

Flexibility and Softness

While strength is important, you also want your macramé cords to have a certain level of flexibility and softness. Flexible cords are easier to manipulate and tie into intricate knots, while softer cords are more comfortable to work with and create a cozy, inviting texture in your finished pieces. Cotton and bamboo cords are known for their softness and flexibility, making them a joy to knot with. Hemp and linen cords may be a bit stiffer at first, but they often soften up with use and washing. Consider the desired drape and movement of your project when selecting cords based on their flexibility and softness.

Color Fastness and Retention

If you're using colored cords in your macramé projects, you'll want to choose ones that have excellent color fastness and retention. This means that the color won't fade, bleed, or transfer onto other cords or surfaces over time, even with exposure to sunlight or washing. Look for cords that have been dyed with high-quality, colorfast dyes, and always follow the manufacturer's care instructions to keep your colors looking vibrant. Some natural fibers, like cotton, may be more prone to fading or bleeding when exposed to sunlight or moisture. If your project will be displayed in a sunny location or may come into contact with water, opt for cords with excellent color fastness to maintain their beautiful hues.

If you're unsure about a cord's color fastness, you can do a simple test by wetting a small piece of the cord and pressing it against a white paper towel - if the color bleeds onto the paper, it may not be the best choice for your project.

Sustainable and Eco-Friendly

As crafters, we have the power to make a positive impact on the environment through the materials we choose. When selecting macramé cords, consider opting for ones that are sustainable and eco-friendly. Look for cords made from organic or recycled fibers, or those that have been produced using environmentally-friendly methods. Many manufacturers now offer cords made from sustainable materials like organic cotton, bamboo, and even recycled plastic bottles. By choosing these eco-conscious options, you can feel good about your macramé projects and know that you're doing your part to support a healthier planet.

Versatility and Compatibility

While it's great to have a go-to cord that you love, it's also important to choose cords that are versatile and compatible with a variety of projects and techniques. Look for cords that can be used for both small and large-scale projects, and those that work well with different knots and patterns. Some cords, like cotton, are incredibly versatile and can be used for a wide range of projects, from delicate jewelry to large-scale wall hangings. Other cords, such as leather or specialty materials, may have more limited applications. Additionally, think about how different cords will work together in a single project. Combining cords of various textures, sizes, and colors can add visual interest and depth to your designs.

Price and Value

Last but not least, consider the price and value of the macramé cords you purchase. While it can be tempting to go for the cheapest option, keep in mind that quality cords will often give you better results and last longer in the long run. That being said, you don't necessarily need to break the bank to get great cords. Look for cords that offer a good balance of quality and affordability, and don't be afraid to shop around and compare prices from different suppliers. Keep in mind that purchasing cords in larger quantities or from wholesale suppliers can often result in lower per-unit costs, making it a smart choice for frequent macramé enthusiasts.

In conclusion, the essential qualities of macramé cords extend beyond just cord materials, thickness, strength and twist. Other essential qualities, such as texture, stiffness, strength, durability, consistency, smoothness, flexibility, softness, color fastness, sustainability, versatility, and value, all play a significant role in determining the overall quality and success of your macramé creations. By keeping these essential qualities in mind, you'll be well on your way to choosing the perfect macramé cords for your projects. Remember, the right cord can make all the difference in the look, feel, and durability of your finished pieces. So take your time, experiment with different fibers and textures, and consider investing in durable cords to ensure long-lasting creations.

3.3.4 Mastering Cord Selection: Making Cord Choices That Last

Having exhaustively examined the foundational elements of macramé cords and considered other salient factors, we now redirect our attention to scrutinize the extrinsic considerations that exert a significant influence on choosing the optimal cord for a particular project. Let's transcend the intrinsic characteristics of cords to investigate how our specific project objectives, environmental circumstances, and pragmatic concerns inform the decision-making process. While the previous chapters focused on understanding what makes each cord unique from a material standpoint, we now shift our attention to the dynamic interplay between these cords and the surrounding environment. It's about identifying the ideal harmony between what a cord inherently possesses and what your project requires to thrive in practical applications.

When selecting a macramé cord, it's crucial to consider the broader context of your project. The **type of project and cord suitability** is our starting point. Envisioning your project type - be it decorative items like wall hangings, functional pieces such as plant hangers, or even wearable art - sets the stage for your craft. Each category demands a specific cord type; for instance, the delicate intricacies of a wall hanging flourish with a softer, more pliable cord, while a plant hanger benefits from a sturdier, more durable material to ensure longevity. This decision impacts not just the aesthetic outcome but also the structural integrity of your creation.

Equally critical is the evaluation of **weight and tensile strength** that involves thinking about the final piece's purpose. These factors are not just abstract measurements but practical indicators of how well a piece will hold up under the weight of its purpose. For decorative items like wall hangings, lighter cords can be beautiful and intricate. However, for functional pieces that will bear weight or endure frequent handling—like plant hangers or bags—opt for cords with higher tensile strength. This ensures they won't stretch out of shape or break under load.

Abrasion resistance further contributes to durability, safeguarding your work against wear and tear from friction or environmental elements. Items like rugs, bags, or outdoor decorations need cords that can withstand friction without fraying or breaking. Look for cords labeled as abrasion-resistant or opt for materials known for their durability, like nylon or thick cotton. Don't hesitate to ask suppliers about the abrasion resistance of their cords or look for reviews from other macramé artists.

Environmental conditions and cord longevity address how external factors such as humidity, sunlight, and temperature fluctuations can affect a cord's appearance and strength over time. If your piece will be displayed outdoors or in areas with high humidity, choose materials that resist moisture and UV damage, like polypropylene or treated cotton. For items in sunlit windows, look for UV-resistant cords to prevent fading. Remember, natural fibers like hemp and untreated cotton can degrade quicker under harsh conditions.

Lastly, **care and maintenance** considerations are essential for ensuring your creation remains pristine over time. Consider how often the item will need cleaning and the practicality of the care process. Natural fibers like cotton are beautiful and soft but may require gentle washing to avoid shrinkage, while synthetic fibers like nylon offer robustness and are easier to clean, often being machine washable. Before making a decision, reflect on the end user's ability to maintain the piece. Opting for a cord that aligns with realistic care expectations will keep your macramé looking its best for years to come.

As we conclude our examination of macramé cords, it's evident that there are numerous factors to take into account other than the physical properties of the materials. The selection process requires a nuanced understanding of both the project's requirements and the cord's capabilities. The true test lies in how well the cord can stand up to the unique demands of each macramé project. This holistic approach not only enhances the aesthetic and structural success of the project but also ensures its longevity and sustainability, crafting creations that are not only visually captivating but also resilient and enduring in the face of their intended purposes and environments. Ultimately, selecting the ideal macramé cord involves a harmonious balance between creativity and technique. It's not just about aesthetics or trends; rather, it's about meticulously planning your project's structure to bring your creative vision to fruition. By considering both the tangible and intangible aspects, you'll create a macramé piece that not only impresses with its beauty but also showcases your thoughtful creativity.

3.4 The Secrets of Estimating Cord Length

When you're lost in the creative flow, it's easy to get caught up in the mesmerizing patterns and stunning color combinations. But have you ever finished a piece only to realize that your cord length was off, leaving you with an unbalanced or incomplete design? Trust me, we've all been there! As a beginner, it's easy to get caught up in the excitement of starting a new project and overlook this essential factor. While the allure of choosing the right materials and achieving stunning visuals can be captivating, truly mastering the art of macramé requires an understanding of the power of cord length. So, why does cord length matter so much? Well, it's simple. The length of your cords not only affects the overall size and scale of your project but also plays a pivotal role in achieving the perfect balance, proportion, drape, and overall appearance of your finished piece. But how do you calculate the perfect cord length? Don't worry, it's not rocket science! Whether you're crafting delicate bracelets or grand wall hangings, there are simple techniques to estimate the required cord length accurately. A little bit of planning goes a long way in saving you time and headaches later on.

3.4.1 How-To Craft Your Personalized Cord Measurement Chart

Imagine having a holy grail of knotting knowledge at your fingertips – a sacred text containing precise cord measurements, tailored to your favorite knots and cord thicknesses. No more guesswork, no more wasted materials – just pure, unadulterated macramé bliss! It's not just a dream—it's a reality waiting to be woven, and it all starts with creating your very own personalized cord measurement chart.

Let's initiate our quest with the beloved Lark's Head knot, the foundation of countless macramé masterpieces. Gather your dowel and your collection of cord thicknesses. Attach a piece of each cord to your dowel, securing it with the elegant Lark's Head knot. Now, make a tiny mark on each cord at the precise point where it emerges from the knot on both ends. With careful precision, untie the knot and measure the distance between those two marks. Voilà! You now possess the exact amount of cord needed to tie a perfect Lark's Head knot with that particular thickness. Record this magical number in your personalized chart, and repeat the process for each cherished cord size in your stash.

But our quest doesn't end there! Next, we turn our attention to the versatile Square Knot — a true chameleon in the macramé realm. Attach two pieces of cord to your dowel using the trusty Lark's Head method, then weave your magic by tying a Square Knot, leaving a small gap between the knot and the dowel. Make marks on the cords at the top and bottom of the knot, like a treasure map leading to macramé gold. Untie the knot, measure each cord (the filler cords will remain the same, but the working cords will differ), and add these precious measurements to your ever-growing chart. Don't be shy about admiring your handiwork! Feeling emboldened? Now, put those cord-wrangling skills to the test by tying a breathtaking pattern of alternating Square Knots. Mark the top and bottom, untie, and measure the result, capturing the essence of these intricate designs in your personalized guide.

This hands-on approach will provide you with a detailed measurement chart, a valuable resource that will grant you a comprehensive understanding of the cord requirements for your favorite macramé designs. By physically tying and untying these complex knot patterns, you'll develop a tactile familiarity with the nuances of each knot, allowing you to anticipate the cord consumption and plan accordingly. This practical experience will empower you to tackle even the most intricate macramé projects with confidence, giving you the skills needed to determine the exact cord lengths required for breathing life into your artistic ideas. So, tie those intricate patterns, measure with care, create your personalized chart and let this experience become a catalyst for your creative growth.

3.4.2 Plan like a Pro: 10 Easy Steps for Perfect Projects

The path to creating intricate knots starts with a single cord, and calculating the right amount of this essential material is the first step toward macramé mastery. This guide unfolds the secrets behind estimating cord length, ensuring your projects start on solid ground and blossom into beautiful creations. So, grab your favorite cup of coffee, and let's cover each detail one at a time until you're a pro at tying knots!

Step 1: Define your project

Identify what you're creating - be it a wall hanging, plant hanger, or another decorative item. Consider what you want it to look like and its purpose. Does it need to bear weight, like a shelf or plant hanger, or is it purely decorative? This will influence the type of cord you choose, based on its strength, flexibility, and aesthetic qualities. This stage is about marrying your creative aspirations with the practicalities of your chosen medium, considering the demands of your project and the capabilities of your cord. It's a phase where dreams begin to take shape, guided by the understanding that the nature of your project dictates the path forward.

Step 2: Sketch your design

Once your project is defined, the next step is to sketch your idea. This isn't merely an artistic exercise but a crucial planning tool. Outline how many cords you'll need, where the knots will go, and how the cords will interact. This step helps estimate the amount of cord needed by visually breaking down the project's structure, including knots, patterns, and the overall design complexity. Also, consider the cord material and thickness at this stage; thicker cords create bulkier knots, which consume more length, and some materials might stretch over time. A well-thought-out sketch not only lays the groundwork for your project but also serves as a reference point, ensuring your creative vision remains aligned with practical execution.

Step 3: Determine the finished length

This isn't about the dimensions of the space it will occupy, but rather the actual size of the piece itself. How long or wide do you want your macramé project to be? This detail is crucial for accurately calculating how much cord you'll need, as it directly impacts the total length of cord required.

Step 4: Choose the right cord

With your project type and sketch in hand, select a cord that matches the demands of your design. Heavier projects require thicker, stronger cords, while decorative pieces might benefit from a variety of thicknesses for texture. Also, remember that natural fibers might stretch, affecting the final length and size. For beginners, cotton cord is forgiving and versatile. Remember, thicker cords make larger knots and require more length; thinner cords do the opposite. The most frequently used cord thicknesses are 3, 4, and 5 mm. For instance, creating three rows of alternating square knots with 3 mm cord will consume significantly less material than crafting the same number of rows using 7 mm cord.

Step 5: Decide on knot types and techniques

Different knots consume different amounts of cord. For example, square knots consume more cord than single Lark's head knots. If your project includes different sections (like a plant hanger with both a pot cradle and a hanging mechanism), plan the knots for each section accordingly. Familiarize yourself with the knots your design requires. Before committing to your final project, practice with small samples to gauge how much cord specific knots and patterns use. This hands-on experience is invaluable for accurate estimation.

Step 6: Account for design and pattern intricacies

The more complex your pattern, the more cord you'll likely need. Intricate designs with dense knotting require extra cord, so it's wise to overestimate slightly to avoid running short.

Step 7: Don't forget fringes and tassels

If your design includes fringes or tassels, add this to your initial cord calculation. These elements can significantly increase the amount of cord needed, especially if they are a prominent feature of your design.

Step 8: Consider your workspace

When planning your macramé project, assess the available workspace. If you have limited space, you may need to adapt the cord length accordingly. For larger projects, it's advisable to measure and segment the cord into manageable sections, making the process more enjoyable and ensuring a seamless flow.

Step 9: Factor in your personal style

The tension with which you secure knots and the intricacy of your patterns directly influence the amount of cord required. Tighter knots and intricate designs often demand a more generous allocation of material. With practice, you'll develop an intuitive understanding of how your technique impacts cord usage. Moreover, spontaneous design flourishes and improvisations are an integral part of the artistic process, adding an organic flair to your pieces. These personal nuances make it imperative to account for your distinctive style when estimating cord requirements. Remain mindful of your knotting habits and adjust your calculations accordingly, ensuring a seamless and satisfying creative experience.

Step 10: Keep records

Document your projects, including the total finished length, the number of cords and their lengths, and any adjustments you made. Keep notes on how much cord you actually used versus what you estimated. This record becomes a goldmine of information for improving the accuracy of your future cord length calculations. This way, you won't have to measure the cord's length all over again. Instead, you can simply refer back to your notes and apply the same tried-and-true formula if you are recreating the same macramé project.

Embrace the learning process

Lastly, acknowledge the learning curve involved in macramé. Your first few projects will be learning experiences. With each project, your understanding of how to accurately estimate cord length will improve, informed by your growing expertise and experience. This path of discovery not only expands your set of skills but also invigorates your creative expression. With each new project, you'll find yourself feeling more confident and capable in your abilities.

Before your project's grand finale, remember: Stack that cord stash—it's better to be looped in extra than caught short!

3.4.3 Macramé Math: Never Run Out of Cord Again!

The absolute worst feeling is reaching the climax of your macramé masterpiece only to realize you're a few inches short of cord. I understand the frustration of running out of cord mid-project. It's like running out of gas mid-road trip, or chocolate mid-binge. We've all been there, and it's not a fun place to be. With a few simple tricks, we can banish the cord demons and ensure smooth sailing (or should I say, knotting!) from start to finish.

1. The Rule of Thumb Method

For those of you who are just dipping your toes into the vast ocean of macramé, let's kick things off with the easy method. For many of our favorite projects like wall hangings and plant hangers, there's a handy rule of thumb that keeps things simple: just take the desired length of your project and multiply it by four. If you plan to fold the cord in half (as you often do for attaching it to a dowel or object with Lark's Head knots), multiply by 2. I know, I know - you might be thinking "But wait! I don't want to do math!". Don't worry, it's simpler than it seems. And once you get the hang of it, you'll be able to eyeball the perfect cord lengths like a pro. Plus, incorporating a little math will enhance your overall creativity and give you newfound freedom in your craft.

Steps:

1. **Determine the Length of the Finished Piece**: Decide the final length from the top of the hanging loop to the bottom of the fringe.

2. **Multiply for Knots & Fringe**: Take this measurement and multiply it by 4 for small projects or 8 for larger projects with more knotting.

3. **Add Extra for Security**: Always add an additional 10-20% to account for variations in knotting tightness and trimming during finishing.

Example

For a simple plant hanger that you want to be 4 inches long:
- Final length: 4 in
- Multiplier for knots/fringe: x4
- Cord length needed (without extra): 4 in * 4 = 16 in
- Extra (20%): 16 in * 0,20 = 3,2 in
- Total Cord Length per strand: 16 in + 3,2 in = 19,2 in
- Multiply the total cord length for the number of strands your design requires: 19,2 in * 8 = 153,6 in (if your design requires 8 strands).

This thumb method is an excellent guide for the majority of macramé projects. However, a ratio of 5 times the project's length may provide more cord for complex or intricate patterns. Conversely, a 3-4 times ratio could suffice for projects with more fringe than knots or basic knot patterns. But what about those intricate pieces where precision is key? When precise measurement in macramé is necessary, you need to account for design factors such as cord size, project complexity, knot patterns, and knot tightness. These factors can significantly influence the required cord length. That's where the precise methods come into play, my detail-oriented artisans!

2. Precise Calculation Method

If you're a visual learner, this method is for you. Grab your cord and practice your knots. This is ideal for intricate patterns, larger projects, or when utilizing expensive or limited materials.

Steps:

1. Create a Small Sample: Knot a small section of your pattern using the cord you plan to use for the project.

2. Measure the Used Cord: Before unraveling, measure the length of the cord that was used for the sample.

3. Measure the Sample's Length: Measure the finished length of the knotted sample.

4. Calculate the Ratio: Divide the used cord length by the finished sample's length. This is your cord-to-project ratio.

5. Determine the Finished Project Size: Estimate the total length of your finished project.

6. Apply the Ratio: Multiply the finished project size by the cord-to-project ratio.

7. Add Extra for Security: As before, add a 10-20% buffer to your total to account for any inconsistencies.

Example:

For an intricate wall hanging	Inches	Meters
Sample used cord	80 in	2 mt
Sample finished length	4 in	0.1 mt
Cord-to-project ratio	80 / 4 = 20	2 / 0.1 = 20
Desired final length of the project	80 in	2 mt
Required cord length without extra	80 * 20 = 1600 in	2 * 20 = 40 mt
Extra (15%)	240 in	6 mt
Total Cord Length	2000 in	46 mt per strand
Number of strands needed	10	10
Total cord needed (meters)	20000 in	460 mt

Remember to consider the number of strands your design requires when calculating the total amount of cord needed. Even if math wasn't your favorite subject in school, don't be intimidated! With a little practice, you'll soon be handling the calculations like a seasoned pro.

3. The Project Breakdown

For more complex macramé projects, such as wall art with intricate patterns, sculptures, or garments, a more precise calculation is necessary. In these cases, I recommend breaking down the project into smaller sections, measuring the cord length for each section, and then adding the lengths together. By following this precise method, you will have the exact cord length for each section of your macramé project.

Steps:

1. Sketch out the design of your project, including all the different sections and patterns. Be sure to include any tassels, fringe, or additional features that will require extra cord length.

2. Measure each section of the design using a ruler or measuring tape, noting the starting and ending points for each section. Be sure to account for any twisted or braided cord sections, as this will affect the overall length.

3. Calculate the cord length for each section based on the number of knots and spacing between rows. Use the following formula for each section: *Cord Length = (Number of Knots x Knot Length) + (Number of Rows x Row Length)*

4. Add the cord lengths for all the sections together, along with any extra length needed for finishing touches such as tassels or fringe.

4. High-Tech Helpers

And for those who have a love affair with tech, there are cord calculator apps and websites that only need you to input your project's parameters. They'll run the numbers and pop out your cord lengths quicker than you can say "double half hitch."

In addition to these meticulous cord length estimation techniques, you may implement the following tools to enhance precision in your macramé projects:

- *Ruler or Measuring Tape*: ensure accurate measurements for each cord, which is essential for every project, whether it's grand or petite.

- *Scissors:* use sharp scissors to make clean, accurate cuts, avoiding unnecessary fraying or uneven lengths.

- *Pen and Paper:* Keep track of cord measurements, ensuring consistency and accuracy throughout your project.

- *Calculator:* Calculations are unavoidable in macramé. Having a calculator handy simplifies the process and helps you avoid errors.

These methods and tools provide the information you need to accurately estimate, measure, and prepare cord lengths for a variety of designs and macramé patterns, enabling you to flawlessly bring your creativity to reality. With this knowledge in hand, you can approach your macramé projects with confidence and precision. Although these methods provide a strong base, one must remember that each knot is distinct and reflects the creative spirit of the individual who crafts it. These methods serve as mere guidelines in the dance of strands and knots. Keep in mind, your role as the artist involves the use of intuition. Don't be afraid to trust your gut when it feels like a piece needs a little more slack, or your heart says "more fringe!" The goal is not just to save you from the dreaded cord shortage, but to empower you to create with confidence and zest. Now, go forth and knot away, secure in the knowledge that you have the power to calculate like a pro. May your cords be plentiful and your knots be true.

3.5 Cutting and Sealing Methods

Prior to beginning the fun part of knotting and creating, there is one final crucial step to complete. After determining the appropriate length of cord for your project, it's essential to cut and prepare the cord properly for use. This process involves cutting and sealing your cords correctly. These simple yet crucial techniques will save you from frustrating frays, running short on cord, and overall macramé mayhem!

First up, cutting. Don't just hack away with any old scissors, darlings. Invest in a sharp, high-quality pair that will slice through those cords like a hot knife through butter. Clean cuts mean no pesky fraying to deal with down the line. When cutting, make sure to cut straight across the cord at a 90-degree angle. This clean, perpendicular cut will help prevent fraying and make it easier to seal the ends.

After cutting the cord to the appropriate length, it's time to seal the ends. Sealing the ends of your cord will prevent fraying and unraveling, which can lead to a messy and unfinished look in your final piece. There are a few different methods you can use to seal your cords, depending on the type of cord you are working with and your personal preference. When working with synthetic cords, a clever technique to keep the ends from fraying is to use a hot knife to melt and seal them. By employing a heated blade, you can effortlessly melt and fuse the synthetic cord, creating a neat and secure finish that will stand the test of time. It's a simple yet ingenious solution.

But what about you, natural fiber enthusiasts, working with cotton, jute and the like? A simple dab of clear nail polish or fabric glue on the cord ends will seal them up tighter than Fort Knox. These liquid sealants can be applied directly to the ends of the cord, where they will dry and form a protective barrier against fraying. Just be sure to let that magical goop dry fully before proceeding. Once you make these easy cut and seal steps a habit, your projects will be smoother, more enjoyable, and entirely stress-free.

No matter your material vice, the key is experimenting until you find that magic formula that works like a charm. Once you've nailed your ideal end-sealing ritual, those frays will be nothing but a faded memory! So go forth and seal those ends with confidence. Your macramé masterpieces are destined to be treasured for many years to come, not unraveling at the first tug. Harness the magic of a polished finish - your walls (and Instagram feeds!) will thank you.

3.6 Care and Maintenance: Longevity of Your Macramé

Crafting those stunning macramé pieces is merely the initial foray into a remarkable undertaking. Just like any meaningful relationship, the connection you have with your macramé requires some TLC to keep it going strong. Think of it this way: you've put your heart and soul into every knot and pattern, so it only makes sense to give your creations the love they deserve, right? So let me let you in on a few simple secrets to keeping your macramé masterpieces looking as fabulous as the day you whipped up that last diagonal knot. With a little bit of love, care, and these handy maintenance tips, you'll be able to create a lasting legacy of beauty and creativity that will be enjoyed for generations to come.

First and foremost, proper **storage** is key to maintaining the quality of your cord. To bid farewell to tangles and frayed ends, the secret lies in the coil. Wrap your cords up nice and neat, then secure them with a twist tie or velcro strap. It's like giving your cords a little hug to keep them safe and sound. You also want a spot that's cool, dry, and away from any pesky sunlight that could fade or weaken those beautiful fibers. Think of it like finding the perfect home for your cords to rest and relax until their next big project. If you're planning on storing your cords for a while, here's a handy trick: grab a pegboard or some hooks and hang those cords up! This keeps them from getting all tangled up or damaged while they wait patiently for you to create your next masterpiece. And don't forget the finishing touch - a cozy dust cloth or some plastic wrap to protect them from any dust bunnies that might come their way. With these simple storage tips, your cords will be ready and raring to go whenever inspiration strikes.

If you're working with a variety of colors or thicknesses, it's a smart idea to store them separately. Nobody wants to spend hours untangling a jumbled mess of cords, right? Clear plastic bins or organizers are a fantastic solution. They'll keep your cords neat, tidy, and easy to find. You'll thank yourself later when you're in the middle of a project and need that perfect shade of blue. And if you want to take your organization game to the next level, consider investing in a cord organizer. These handy little devices will keep your cords from getting tangled and make it a breeze to find the one you need. Another simple trick is to use labeled ziplock bags or small containers for each color. It may seem like a small detail, but it can make a big difference in your crafting experience. Remember, a well-organized cord collection is a thing of beauty. It'll save you time, frustration, and a whole lot of headaches.

When working on a macramé project, it's all about treating those cords with a little TLC so, **handle** your cords with care. First off, be gentle with your movements. No need to yank or tug too hard - slow and steady wins the race! Rough handling can really do a number on those fibers over time. Another thing to watch out for is friction. Try to steer clear of any abrasive surfaces that might wear down your cords prematurely. And if you're threading them through a tight spot, take it easy! Forcing them through can cause some serious strain. The key is to take your time with each step of the process. Give every knot and loop your full attention, making sure everything is just right. By handling your materials with care, you'll keep those cords strong and resilient.

Another crucial aspect of cord maintenance is regular **cleaning**. Start by dusting your creations regularly with a gentle brush or duster and give your macramé a gentle once-over. This will help keep dirt and grime from settling into those gorgeous knots. If you want to take it a step further, use a hairdryer on a cool, low setting to blow away any stubborn dust particles. If a pesky stain or spot appears, just mix up a mild detergent or gentle soap with some water, and dab the stain with a clean cloth. Be careful not to scrub too hard, or you might damage the fibers. Rinse the area with clean water and pat it dry with a towel. For a deeper clean, fill a basin with lukewarm water and a small amount of gentle detergent. Let your macramé soak for about 15-20 minutes, then gently swish it around to loosen any dirt. Rinse it thoroughly with clean water and squeeze out the excess moisture. Lay your piece flat to dry, but keep it out of direct sunlight. Want to keep your cords soft and supple? Try adding a fabric softener to the rinse cycle. This will help prevent the fibers from getting stiff or brittle over time. Remember, different cord materials may require specific care instructions, so be sure to check the guidelines for your particular project.

Preserving the splendor of your handcrafted macramé pieces is just as crucial as keeping them clean. To prevent dust and dirt from accumulating on your creations when not in use, store them in a breathable cotton bag or hang them in a dry, shaded spot. Steer clear of exposing your macramé to harsh chemicals, direct sunlight, or excessive moisture, as these can weaken the fibers and lead to deterioration over time. If your piece features tassels or fringe, take care to protect them from tangling or unraveling by gently combing them out with a wide-toothed comb. To keep your macramé art looking brand-new, you can also consider applying a fabric protector spray to help repel dirt and stains. Remember to test the spray on a small, inconspicuous area first to ensure it won't cause any discoloration or damage. For added freshness, use a fabric freshener spray to keep your macramé art smelling clean and inviting. If you have plant hangers that are in constant contact with moisture and soil, it's essential to regularly check for mold or mildew. Should you notice any signs of mold growth, remove the affected plant hanger immediately and wash it according to the care instructions. You can also consider spraying a mixture of vinegar and water on the affected area to help prevent further mold growth.

When **storing** your macramé projects, make sure to hang them up whenever possible. You don't want to risk your hard work getting all tangled up or losing its shape. A sturdy hook or hanger will do the trick, keeping your pieces off the ground and safe from any potential damage. I know hanging isn't always an option, and that's okay! If you need to store your macramé projects in a bin or drawer, just make sure to fold them carefully and wrap each piece in some tissue paper or fabric. This will create a protective barrier between your creations and prevent any unwanted tangling. And remember, don't overload that storage container! You don't want to crush or distort those beautiful designs you've worked so hard on. Another important thing to keep in mind is where you're storing your macramé. Direct sunlight and heat sources? No way! Prolonged exposure to sunlight can fade those vibrant colors, while heat can weaken the fibers and cause them to break. Stick to a cool, dry place to keep your creations looking their best. If you're planning on storing your macramé projects for a longer period, consider investing in a protective bag or garment cover. This will shield your pieces from dust and dirt, keeping them looking fresh and new. Just make sure the bag is made of a breathable material like cotton or linen to allow for air circulation and prevent any moisture buildup that could lead to mold or mildew growth. No one wants that!

Over time, the ends of your macramé cords may start to fray. To prevent further unraveling, trim any frayed ends with sharp scissors. Be sure to cut as close to the fray as possible without cutting any additional threads. After trimming, you can apply a small amount of clear nail polish or fabric glue to the end of the cord to prevent further fraying. Allow the polish or glue to dry completely. Another handy trick for repairing frayed cords is to use a small amount of heat to seal the ends. If you have a longer snag in your cord that you can't simply trim away, you can try gently pulling the surrounding threads to close the gap. Use a small crochet hook or a pair of tweezers to carefully work the snag back into place.

Lastly, remember to regularly **inspect** your macramé creations for any signs of wear and tear, such as loose knots or fraying fibers. If you spot any issues, don't hesitate to jump into action and make the necessary repairs right away to prevent further damage. For those of you rocking some gorgeous macramé plant hangers, regular check-ups are an absolute must. Over time, the ropes or cords holding up your precious plants can start to weaken, especially if they're exposed to a lot of sunlight or moisture. Nobody wants their plants taking a nosedive because of a broken cord!

Caring for your macramé creations with intention can breathe new life into them. By tending to these sacred rituals, you can extend the lifespan of your pieces and retain their artistry and charm for generations to come, enriching your living spaces with timeless beauty. These pieces can become treasured heirlooms to be passed down through generations, leaving a lasting legacy. As you pass your cherished macramé down through the generations, you're not only sharing a beautiful object— you're gifting a piece of your heart and leaving a lasting legacy of creativity. Your dedication to this craft will be forever woven into the fabric of your family's story, connecting you to loved ones across time.

3.7 Color & Dye Methods

The art of dyeing macramé cords unlocks a tapestry of opportunities, enabling you to instill your projects with the very essence of your creativity. It's a process that transcends the bounds of technique, transforming the humble cord into a medium for self-expression. You'll investigate the principles of color theory, understanding how different pigments interact and blend to create your desired palette.

Understanding the types of dyes and their application methods is the first step in this colorful adventure. The choice between natural and synthetic dyes is akin to selecting the path that resonates most with your personal aesthetic and environmental values. Natural dyes, extracted from the bountiful resources of plants, minerals, and even insects, offer a palette that echoes the timeless hues of nature. These earthy tones not only connect you with the ancient traditions of textile coloring but also embrace an eco-friendly approach to your craft. Surrounded by a tapestry of terrestrial hues, you'll become fully engaged in a universe where the earth's vibrant colors infuse your macramé creations with a sense of warmth and authenticity. Imagine the calming tranquility of indigo blues, the inviting warmth of ochre yellows, and the lively vitality of madder reds – each shade a reflection of the natural landscape. On the other hand, the realm of artificial pigments reveals an infinite palette of colors. From delicate pastels to the most radiant shades imaginable, this path ensures that every color you've ever dreamed of is within your grasp. Synthetic dyes offer consistency and durability, making them a go-to choice for projects that demand long-lasting brilliance.

Selecting the ideal dye initiates a fascinating pursuit of converting ordinary cords into vibrant, eye-catching works of art. But hold on tight, because the real magic is about to unfold! Preparing the dye bath is where the excitement truly begins. It's like concocting a secret potion, where you blend the perfect ingredients to create a mesmerizing elixir of color. First, fill a pot with water and heat it until it's just below boiling point. As the water simmers, carefully add your chosen dye, stirring gently to ensure even distribution. The key to achieving a consistent color is to maintain the right water temperature and dye concentration throughout the process. Before you start, take a moment to understand your fabric's unique personality. Each material has its own quirks and absorption properties, so getting to know your cords is key to achieving that perfect shade. It's time to submerge your cords into the dye bath, making sure they're fully immersed. The longer you let them soak, the more intense and saturated the color will become. It's like watching a mesmerizing dance as the dye gradually penetrates the fibers, animating them with each passing second. Creating the perfect shade is not just about following a recipe; it's about trusting your instincts and letting your creativity shine. As you patiently wait, the anticipation builds. Will the final result match your vision? The beauty of hand-dyeing lies in its unpredictability – each piece becomes a unique creation, bearing the mark of your artistic touch. Finally, when the desired hue is achieved, carefully remove the cords from the dye bath and rinse them thoroughly under cool water. As the excess dye washes away, you'll see the true depth of those luscious shades finally emerge. It's like watching a butterfly slowly unfurl its wings after its metamorphosis. With each gentle squeeze, more of that rich, even color blooms across the strands. Then comes the drying phase, a period of delicious anticipation as you carefully arrange your handiwork and wait for the final reveal. With each passing hour, the cords drink in the last rays of color until they reach peak vibrancy. And when you finally run those buttery-soft, saturated strands through your fingers? Pure macramé nirvana. It's a moment that will take your breath away. It's not just about the visual impact, though that's certainly part of the magic. It's about recognizing the love, skill, and dedication you've poured into your craft. From the moment you carefully select the perfect dye to the final reveal of your transformed cords, you're undertaking a path that intertwines the precision of science with the soul of art, where meticulous care and creative passion converge.

As you further pursue the art of dyeing macramé cords, you'll discover that the opportunities are truly limitless. From ombré effects to color blocking, from subtle gradients to bold contrasts, each technique presents a fresh opportunity to exhibit your artistic flair and uncover new aesthetics. I know the thought of transforming those plain fibers into a kaleidoscope of hues may seem intimidating at first. Start small. Opt for mini projects and mellow shades as you dip your toes into this colorful pool. Play and experiment shamelessly - grab those dye pots and sample cords, letting each trial teach and inspire you. Before you know it, you'll be a dyeing diva, confidently breathing new life into gorgeous macramé masterpieces.

When it comes to selecting the perfect palette for your macramé masterpiece, envision your macramé creation as a blank canvas eagerly awaiting your artistic touch. Each hue you choose has the power to evoke a specific emotion, set a desired mood, and effortlessly complement the existing décor of your space. The colors you opt for can set the entire vibe - whether you're going for a relaxing beachy feel with sandy neutrals or a bold, vibrant look that screams "Girls just wanna have fun!". If you're drawn to the soothing simplicity of a single shade, a monochromatic approach can look absolutely stunning. Whatever your vision, run with it! Savor the thrill of experimentation, blending, and contrasting, unearthing surprising pairings that ignite your passion. At the end of the day, there's no such thing as a "wrong" color choice. Trust your instincts and let your creativity flow freely.

As we immerse ourselves in the rich tapestry of colors, let's not forget to consider the ecological footprint that accompanies our investigation. Choosing natural dyes and sustainable practices isn't just eco-friendly – it's a way to imbue your crafting with more mindfulness and meaning. Your wall hanging or plant hanger won't just adorn a space – it will emanate the values and visions you've woven into every knot and hue becoming a reflection of your commitment to a more sustainable, mindful way of creating. A labor of love, crafted in harmony with nature's rhythms. As you set out on this path of conscious crafting, know that you are not alone. A growing community of like-minded artisans is embracing this eco-friendly approach, and together, we can inspire others to follow suit. By sharing our knowledge, experiences, and beautiful creations, we can spark a ripple effect of positive change in the arena of macramé and further afield.

So have no fear and just be prepared to take the leap and initiate a vibrant undertaking that will forever alter the way you approach your macramé projects. Play with color like a kid with a new box of crayons. Mix hues with reckless abandon. After all, any "mistakes" just add delightfully rich character. This dynamic quest is all about unleashing your unique talents and inner voice, one gloriously hand-dyed cord at a time. The vibrant palette of color awaits, and your cords are ready to be transformed into something spectacular.

Chapter 4: The Beginner's Route from Basic Knots to Advanced Techniques

Step into the core of macramé mastery! This chapter will guide you through the fundamental techniques and crucial knots that will elevate your cord into a magnificent piece of art. We'll study the active Lark's Head and Half Hitch knots, exploring the variations of each method, alongside the widely recognized Square Knot. You'll also learn how to add texture, dimension, and sparkle to your creations using special knots, beads, and fringe.

4.1 Lark's Head Knot and Its Variations

The Lark's Head Knot is a fundamental technique in macramé and its versatility makes it one of the most commonly used knots. This simple yet secure knot allows you to attach cords to rings or create decorative knot patterns. While the basic Lark's Head is easy to master, there are several creative variations that open up endless design possibilities.

Lark's Head Knot: Often the starting point for many macramé projects, this knot is used to attach your cord to the dowel, ring, or another piece of cord. It's foundational and versatile.

Vertical Lark's Head Knot: A variation that creates a different texture and pattern, often used in wall hangings and plant hangers for decorative effect.

Continuous Lark's Head Knot: This method involves creating a series of Lark's Head Knots without cutting the cord, producing a continuous decorative pattern.

Alternating Lark's Head Knot: By alternating the direction or placement of each knot, this variation offers a way to create intricate patterns and textures in your piece.

Lark's Head Knot Picot: A decorative adaptation, combining the Lark's Head with a picot technique to add delicate details to your work.

4.2 Half Hitch Knot and Its Variations

The humble half hitch knot is the building block for countless macramé designs. Despite its simplicity, this versatile knot holds unlimited potential through creative variations. From textured waves to intricate lacework, a landscape of knotted artistry unfolds for those who dare to immerse themselves.

Half Hitch: This simple knot can be used to create lines, borders, and shapes within macramé pieces. It's fundamental for adding detail and texture.

Alternating Half Hitch: This variation involves alternating the direction of the Half Hitches to create complex patterns and textures.

Double Half Hitch: Builds on the Half Hitch by using two consecutive hitches. It's essential for creating lines and shapes, acting as a building block for patterns.

Horizontal Half Hitch Knot: Horizontal lines of Half Hitches can form patterns or secure sections of work. It's a versatile decorative element.

Vertical Half Hitch Knot: Similar to the horizontal version but worked vertically, it's used for adding texture and pattern along the length of a piece.

Half Hitch Knot with Waves: By varying the tension and spacing of the Half Hitch, you can create undulating patterns that mimic waves, adding movement to your work.

4.3 Square Knot and Its Variations

The square knot is a fundamental knot in macramé, forming the basis for many intricate designs. Its simplicity belies its versatility - with just a few twists, this humble knot can be transformed into an array of eye-catching variations. From the delicate half knot to the sturdy square knot sinnet, each variation adds depth, texture and visual interest.

Half Knot: A simple knot that twists to create a spiral effect. It's the basis for the Spiral Knot and can be used to add texture or decorative elements.

Square Knot: A foundational macramé knot used in a wide variety of projects. It's created by combining two Half Knots and is essential for building patterns.

Alternating Square Knot: By offsetting the Square Knots, this variation adds dimension and interest, creating a mesh or net-like effect.

Square Knot Sinnet: A series of Square Knots tied in succession, creating a strong, decorative column or band. It's great for adding structure to your pieces.

Square Knot Picot: Incorporating picot loops into Square Knots introduces decorative edging and detail, perfect for finishing touches or added intricacy.

4.4 Special Knots for Texture and Decoration

Macramé knots are the building blocks of this intricate art form, each with its own unique charm and purpose. From the intricate Spiral Knot to the eye-catching Berry Knot, these knotting methods have been around for ages, adding that extra "oomph" to everything from wall art to plant hangers and even jewelry. Whether you're creating a whimsical Wall Hanging or a sturdy Key Chain, the versatility of knots like the Wrap Knot, Square Button Knot, and Rose Knot allows you to express your creativity while crafting pieces that are both beautiful and functional.

Spiral Knot: A foundational technique that creates a twisted, rope-like effect, adding texture and visual interest.

Berry Knot: Creates a textured, bobbled effect, perfect for adding decorative elements to your pieces.

Wrapping Knot: A method for securing a group of cords together, ideal for finishing touches or structural elements.

Square Button Knot or Rose Knot: Often used as decorative elements, these knots add a floral or geometric aesthetic to your projects.

Josephine Knot: A beautiful, intricate knot that resembles a twisted figure-eight, adding elegance and complexity.

Crown Knot: A versatile knot used for creating a rounded structure, ideal for basket handles and decorative spirals.

Pipa Knot: Named for its resemblance to the Chinese lute (pipa), this knot adds a unique, elegant touch to any project.

Monkey Fist Knot: Originally used as a weight at the end of a rope, it's now popular in macramé for creating spherical accents.

Chinese Good Luck Knot: A traditional knot symbolizing good luck and prosperity, intricate and often used as a pendant or decoration.

Triangle Knot: Used to create triangular patterns or as a decorative element, adding geometric diversity.

Barrel Knot: A simple yet versatile knot that can be used for adding texture or as spacers between beads.

Cat's Paw Knot: A hitching type of knot that creates a compact, paw-like shape, adding interesting texture.

Endless Falls Knot: A repetitive knotting technique that creates a cascading effect, ideal for wall hangings or plant hangers.

4.5 Perfecting Finishes with Ending Knots

The final touches can make all the difference in your macramé masterpieces. Perfecting the ending knots is key to maintain the aesthetic appeal and durability of your projects. The ending knots hold everything together and give your piece a polished, professional look. Take the time to perfect these final knots, and your macramé will impress everyone who sees it.

Barrel Knot: Ideal for creating a strong, decorative end, the Barrel Knot is perfect for finishing bracelets or necklaces, ensuring the cords are secure and the transition to clasps is both smooth and aesthetically pleasing.

Heaving Line Knot: Though traditionally used to add weight, when applied as an ending knot, it provides a visually striking and bulky end, perfect for adding a statement finish to wall hangings or keychains.

Leaf Knot: While primarily decorative, ending a piece with a Leaf Knot adds a delicate, naturalistic touch. This can be especially effective in pieces where a thematic closure mirrors the design's overall motif.

Figure 8 Knot: Simple yet strong, the Figure 8 Knot is an excellent choice for ending lines where security is paramount. Its ease of tying and untying makes it practical for adjustable or temporary installations.

Gathering Knot: A quintessential finish for many macramé pieces, the Gathering Knot is not only secure but also offers a neat, cohesive look by encapsulating multiple strands. It's ideal for the final tie-off in wall hangings and plant hangers.

4.6 Combining Knots for Complex Patterns

At its heart, macramé is about knots. However, the true artistry emerges when these knots are repeated in thoughtful patterns. This repetition forms the backbone of your design, bringing about a seamless transformation from simple strands to intricate works of art. Every great macramé piece starts with an understanding of basic knots and techniques. Think of basic macramé knots as your alphabet. Just as letters combine to form words, knots like the square knot, double half hitch, and spiral knot become the building blocks of intricate patterns. Mastering these fundamental knots is key to unlocking a broad panorama of design possibilities. Repeating a single knot can create stunning textures. For instance, rows of alternating square knots form the classic flat braid, while rows of double half hitches yield the elegant spiral stitch. Here are some ideas to spark your creativity:

- **Vertical Patterns**: Alternate rows of different knots or combine them to form vertical stripes and geometric designs.
- **Horizontal Patterns**: Create horizontal bands using alternating knot sequences or incorporate picots for a touch of delicate charm.
- **Diagonal Patterns**: Utilize diagonal clove hitch variations to form chevron patterns or experiment with alternating half hitch knots to add a dynamic flair.

While repetition is key, don't be afraid to break the pattern occasionally. Introduce intentional "mistakes" or variations to add a touch of individuality to your work. This can be as simple as changing the the size, tension, color or direction of your knots, adding a unique embellishment, varying the number of cords used in each section or even combining macramé with other fiber arts like weaving or crochet for truly unique creations. The key is to find a balance between repetition and variation to keep your design interesting and visually engaging.

Understanding spacing is another crucial aspect. Spacing in a macramé pattern determines the flow of the piece. It's like the timing in music – too rushed, and the piece feels chaotic; too slow, and it may seem dull. Learning to adjust knot spacing according to the pattern's suggestion, while also considering the type of cord or yarn you're using, is key to ensuring your creation breathes just the right way. Additionally, maintaining an even tension on your cords is crucial to ensure uniformity.

Mastering pattern repetition will give you a powerful tool to elevate your macramé creations, adding a layer of sophistication and visual appeal. So, gather your cords, pick your favorite knots, and let the rhythmic dance of pattern play begin!

4.7 Mounting Techniques

Mounting is a critical step in the macramé process, and it's an area where many artists struggle, especially when they are first starting out. In macramé, "mounting" essentially refers to how you secure your work to a support structure, such as dowels, rings, or branches. This foundational step isn't just about practicality—it sets the stage for your entire piece, influencing both its form and its function. A well-mounted piece holds better under tension, allowing more complex designs to keep their shape and strength over time.

The first step to a polished macramé piece is understanding how to start and secure your knots effectively. Securing the knot is an essential step in the macramé process and is the foundation of your entire creation. Think of it as laying the first bricks of a house; if they're not placed securely, the entire structure is at risk. Macramé artists use a variety of knots to start their projects and secure the cordage, ensuring the design remains intact and durable. One of the most popular and versatile starting knots is the **lark's head knot**. This knot creates a secure loop that can be attached to a ring, dowel, or any other mounting hardware you choose. For extra security, especially when working with thicker cords or heavier projects, a **double half-hitch knot** can be added below the lark's head. This combination provides a firm anchor that will keep your cords in place and prevent any unwanted unravelling. Another important knot for securing your work is the **gathering knot**. This is used to group cords together and create a secure anchor point for your design. It is especially useful when working with multiple cords and wanting to keep them organized and in place. For fabric-wrapped forms or unconventional bases, **sewing or using fabric glue** can be excellent options. Just ensure your chosen adhesive is suitable for the materials you're using.

Another popular mounting technique is using a **wooden dowel**. This method involves attaching the top of your macramé piece to a wooden dowel using a simple lark's head knot. The wooden dowel can then be hung on a wall using a nail or hook, allowing your macramé creation to hang beautifully and be the focal point of the room. This method is perfect for larger pieces and creates a clean and polished look. You can also experiment with different types of wooden dowels to add a unique twist to your macramé design. For a more decorative mounting option, consider using a **metal hoop**. Slide the hoop through the loops at the top of your macramé piece and attach it securely. This technique works well for creating a modern and minimalist look, and you can choose from a variety of hoop sizes adding a modern and industrial touch to your macramé creations.. If you want to add a touch of nature to your macramé piece, try mounting it on a **driftwood branch**. Driftwood branches can add a natural and bohemian feel to your macramé creations. Simply attach the top of your macramé piece to the driftwood branch using knots or strings, and then hang the branch on a wall using a sturdy hook or rope. For those who prefer a minimalist look, mounting your macramé creations on a **copper pipe** can be a great option. Simply slide the top of your macramé piece onto the copper pipe and hang it on the wall using hooks or brackets. The copper pipe adds a sleek and modern touch to your macramé creation while keeping the focus on the intricate knotting and design. For those with advanced macramé skills, a **macramé board** may be the perfect mounting option. Macramé boards are specially designed boards with grid patterns that allow for precise knotting and intricate designs. By securing your piece to a macramé board, you can create complex patterns and designs with ease, making it an ideal choice for detailed wall hangings or tapestries.

No matter your skill level, there are creative ways to secure your macramé creations that will enhance their beauty and ensure they are displayed securely. Before selecting a mounting technique, take a close look at your macramé piece. Consider the size, shape, and weight of the project. Larger, heavier pieces may require more robust mounting techniques, while smaller, lighter pieces can be mounted with simpler methods. By investigating different mounting techniques such as wooden dowels, metal hoops, driftwood branches, and macramé boards, you can find the ideal approach to showcase your macramé artistry in style.

Now comes the exciting part – displaying your creation for all to admire! Here are some unique ways to showcase your creations:

- **Rings, Hoops, and Decorative Rods**: Opt for elegance and sophistication by displaying your macramé on wooden or metal rings, or elegant decorative rods with finials. Choose materials and colors that complement your piece, adding a touch of refinement to your design.

- **Macramé Hoop**: Experiment with mounting your creation on a macramé hoop, adding an unexpected geometric element to your décor. This unique approach will draw the eye and showcase your craft in a new light.

- **Delicate Display**: For a whimsical touch, use ribbons to hang your macramé. Coordinating ribbons provide a subtle, soft look, perfect for a dreamy, romantic aesthetic.

- **Modern Minimalism**: Consider a floating frame to showcase your macramé. This contemporary display method highlights your artwork against a blank canvas, drawing focus to the intricate knots and textures.

- **Simple Solutions**: Sometimes, simple is best. A decorative wall hook provides an effortless mounting option, perfect for smaller pieces or as part of a gallery wall display.

- **Bohemian Vibe**: Embrace the bohemian trend by displaying multiple macramé hangings on a decorative ladder. This eclectic approach adds instant visual interest to any room, creating a unique and cozy atmosphere.

- **Temporary Twist**: If you're renting or prefer a changeable display, opt for a tension rod. This versatile option allows for easy swapping of your macramé without committing to wall holes.

The foundation of any good macramé piece lies in the knots, so take pride in mastering those starting points and revel in the limitless possibilities of showcasing your creations. Whether you opt for a simple ring or an eclectic ladder display, each creation will take on a life of its own, reflecting your unique style and the beauty of knots in motion. Keep creating, experimenting, and share your incredible macramé masterpieces with the globe!

4.8 Textures and Twists for Dimensional Designs

Leave your basic knots behind, because we're interlacing a global expanse of 3D enchantment where your macramé pieces will truly come alive and pop off the wall. We're departing from the flat and launching into the arena of texture and twists – where your macramé creations burst forth with captivating depth and dimension. Forget the "one-dimensional wall hanging" stereotype; we're about to elevate your macramé game. Dimensional design is like *"the Beyoncé"* of macramé. It adds depth, sass, and a touch of "Who run the world?" confidence. The key to this fibre domination is all about playing with different knots, materials, and, of course, textures.

Remember those basic knots you mastered? Well, get ready to see them in a whole new light. By introducing simple twists and turns to your foundational knots, you unlock a universe of textural possibilities.

- **The Square Knot Remix**: Instead of working with your cords flat, try adding a half-twist before tying each knot. This creates a beautiful spiraling effect, adding dynamic movement to your piece.
- **Spiral Knot Magic**: This knot is a textural wonder on its own, but experiment with different cord thicknesses and tension to create varying degrees of tightness and looseness.
- **The Josephine Knot**: This intricate knot is a textural powerhouse, with its braided appearance adding a touch of elegance and complexity.

Think outside the knot! There's a vast array of tactile methods simply begging to be investigated. Incorporating texture into your macramé can transform a flat, two-dimensional piece into a tactile, inviting work of art. To achieve these stunning effects, it's important to experiment with different materials and techniques. Cotton, jute, and even recycled materials can all be used to create unique and visually striking pieces. And don't be afraid to play with color, either — bold hues and subtle gradients can add an extra layer of depth and visual interest to your macramé.

Here are some of my favorite techniques to add dimension and drama to your work:

- **Knot Variations**: Start simple. The kind of knots you choose can dramatically change the texture of your piece. Alternating between square knots and spiral knots, for instance, creates a delightful rhythm that draws the eye along the pattern. Knots like the square knot or the half-hitch can be manipulated to create interesting patterns. For instance, repeating square knots in alternating directions builds a neat, compact pattern, while diagonal half-hitches create sweeping lines that draw the eye across your design. For a different texture, consider using clove hitches to create textured rows that add a subtle, layered effect to your piece. Be adventurous with combining different knots to see how they interact with each other.

- **Layering Patterns for Depth**: Layering different knot patterns is like layering fabrics: it adds richness and depth. You can create a base layer using a dense pattern like the double half-hitch and overlay it with more open knots like the Josephine knot. The juxtaposition of dense and airy patterns gives a piece visual intrigue. To avoid a cluttered look, stick to a limited palette of knots and alternate them thoughtfully, creating a rhythm that draws the eye from top to bottom.

- **Looping and Weaving**: Loops aren't just functional; they can be a stunning decorative feature. Try leaving some loose loops of thread in strategic places or weaving portions of your cords back into the design at different points to create bulges, waves, or curls that stand out.

- **Varying Cord Thickness**: This can have a surprisingly profound impact. Experiment with different thicknesses in the same piece to promote contrast. Thicker cords make your work feel more robust and can provide a 'frame' for more delicate, intricate sections made with thinner cords.

- **Incorporating Color**: Color inherently adds depth. Layering lighter colors atop darker hues or interspersing bright flashes of color can give the illusion of foreground and background, making your design pop.

- **Embracing Negative Space**: Negative space, or the empty spaces between knots, plays a crucial role in dimensional design. By leaving certain areas of your macramé pattern open, you can emphasize the parts that are filled with intricate knots and textures. Experiment with varying the density of knots in different sections, using open spaces to contrast and highlight more complex patterns. This technique creates depth by making the filled areas stand out more boldly against their empty neighbors.

Incorporating textures and twists into macramé designs can introduce a new dimension, enhancing the interplay between knots, materials, and negative space and fostering endless creativity. This practice, however, extends beyond mere aesthetics. Textures and twists also have practical benefits; for example, adding texture can protect the hands from the friction of the rope during the knotting process, thereby increasing comfort. Furthermore, utilizing thicker ropes can bolster the strength and durability of the finished pieces. Mixing materials like leather cords, cotton, and wool threads also creates an interesting interplay of textures. Think about how different materials will feel and look together. Adding a wooden or metal ring in the center of your design can serve as a focal point, anchoring the composition and adding dimension.

But wait, there's more! While knots and cord variations lay the groundwork for stunning dimensional designs, we can elevate our creations even further with some extra embellishments. The next two chapters will provide an in-depth examination of the world of *Beads and Baubles and Fringe and Tassels*, showing you how to incorporate these eye-catching elements into your macramé masterpieces. Get ready to add sparkle, movement, and even more personality to your work!

4.9 Incorporating Beads and Embellishments

We've mastered the knots, wrestled with cord, and birthed beautiful macramé pieces. Now, it's time to enter the shimmering universe of beads and baubles. These little gems are like the sprinkles on our macramé cupcake, adding pops of color, texture, and personality. Macramé and beads are like peanut butter and jelly - they just work so well together! Beads add an extra layer of detail and interest, and can really make your macramé projects stand out. From boho chic to elegant sophistication, beads can help you achieve any style you desire.

Firstly, selecting the right beads is crucial. They come in a myriad of shapes, sizes, materials, and colors. From tiny glass seed beads to chunky wooden ones, each brings its unique charm. The size and shape of the bead will depend on the type of knot and pattern you're using. It's important to choose beads that not only look great but are also appropriate for your project. Remember, the bead should easily slide over your cord but be secure once knotted.

When it comes to adding beads to your macramé, the most common method is the "**bead-stringing**" technique. It's simple yet effective. You'll thread your beads onto your cord before you begin your knotting pattern. Once the beads are in place, you'll knot around them, securing each one in its designated spot. For a more intricate look, you might want to try the "**bead-weaving**" technique. This method involves weaving the beads into your knots as you go along, creating a beautifully complex pattern. It's a bit more challenging but well worth the effort.

The first method works best for projects with a repeating pattern, while the second approach is ideal for random or more intricate designs. Other methods for incorporating beads include:

- **Alternating Beads**: For a more intricate pattern, alternate beads between different cords. This method creates a stunning, symmetrical design perfect for plant hangers or wall art.
- **Fringe Beading**: Add beads to the fringe at the bottom of your design for extra flair. Thread beads onto the fringe cords and tie a knot at the end to secure them. This is an excellent way to add a playful touch to larger macramé pieces.
- **Cluster Beading**: Create clusters by threading multiple beads onto several cords and securing them with knots. This technique works wonderfully for creating focal points in your designs, adding an artistic touch to your work.

Here are some tips for successfully incorporating beads into your macramé:

- **Pre-stringing**: If you're pre-stringing your beads, it's essential to measure your cords accurately to ensure that you have enough length for the number of beads you plan to use.
- **Bead placement**: Make sure to place your beads evenly throughout your design, taking into account any patterns or focal points you want to create.
- **Securing beads**: When adding beads as you go, it's important to secure them in place with tight knots to prevent them from shifting around.

- **Mix and match**: Don't be afraid to mix and match different types, sizes, and colors of beads to create a unique and eye-catching design.
- **Experiment**: Try incorporating beads in various ways, such as using them as accents or creating entire sections of beaded patterns. Your creativity is the limit!

As you weave the final bead into place and secure your knots, take a moment to appreciate the intricate dance of cords and beads that has unfolded before you. Each bead, with its unique sparkle and story, has become an integral part of your macramé tapestry, weaving tales that only your heart truly knows. As the beads bask in the light and cast their captivating reflections, allow yourself to marvel at the beautiful art you've created. But wait, your artistic trajectory is far from complete! In our next chapter, we'll venture into the captivating universe of macramé fringe and tassels, where whimsical wisps and playful strands eagerly await your creative touch. Get ready to learn how these delightful elements can bring movement, depth, and a touch of bohemian flair to your designs.

4.10 Adding Flair with Fringe and Tassels

Fringe and Tassels: these playful additions are like the exclamation points of the macramé universe. More than just finishing touches, they infuse your creations with movement, texture, and personality.

Fringe is a type of decorative trim made up of strands or threads that dangle down from the edge of your design. It adds movement and dimension, drawing attention to the piece and making it more eye-catching. You can use it on plant hangers, wall hangings, or even as a border on a tablecloth. Think of fringe as the sassy little sister of macramé. It's carefree, it's fun, and it knows how to shake things up! Adding fringe to your macramé isn't just about aesthetics (although, let's face it, they're pretty fabulous on that front). They can modify the texture and flow of your pieces, giving your work a dynamic that is both visually appealing and tactile. Whether it's a wall hanging that whispers secrets when caught in a breeze, or a plant hanger that flirts with every flutter, fringes add movement and character to your creations.

Tassels, on the other hand, are like the glamorous cousins who always steal the show. These charming little additions can be attached at the ends of cords or yarn for a distinctive touch. They come in all shapes, sizes, and colors and add a touch of elegance and sophistication.
To create a fringe, you typically finish off a row of macramé knots and leave the remaining threads long. These can be combed out to a fluffy elegance or trimmed evenly for a tidy, chic edge. For tassels, wrap your chosen thread around a piece of cardboard to the length you desire, slide the loop off, tie off one end and cut the other—voila, you've got yourself a tassel!

Now, attaching these elements can enhance various areas of your work. They can be added to any part of your macramé project, but are typically used at the edges of a piece to add movement and texture. You might line the bottom of a piece with a neat row of tassels or sporadically place them throughout a larger wall hanging to create points of interest. The placement can influence not only the design balance but also how the piece interacts with surroundings. The beauty of fringe and tassels lies in their versatility. You can leave them long and flowing for a bohemian vibe, or trim them into geometric shapes for a modern twist. Play with different thicknesses and textures of cord to create contrast and visual interest. And don't be afraid to get creative with color! A pop of vibrant yarn at the end of a neutral fringe can completely transform a piece. You can even dye your own fringe to achieve a truly unique look. Remember, the way you finish your fringes or tassels can be as creative as the project itself. Use beads, dye sections of your fringes, or even incorporate braiding. These finishing touches not only secure the threads but add an extra layer of design sophistication.

There are countless ways to incorporate fringe and tassels into your macramé projects, but here are a few of my favorites:

- The Classic Fringe: This simple technique involves leaving the warp cords uncut at the bottom of your piece. You can then trim them to your desired length and shape.
- The Wrapped Fringe: Take your fringe up a notch by wrapping a contrasting color of cord around the top portion. This adds a pop of color and helps to prevent fraying.
- The Tassel Trio: Create a cluster of tassels in varying sizes and attach them to a ring or bar for a playful and eye-catching accessory.

- The Beaded Tassel: Elevate your tassels by adding beads, charms, or other embellishments.

Here are a few tips for working with fringe and tassels:

- Choose the right length: The length of your fringe or tassels will have a big impact on the final look of your piece. Choose a length that complements the size and scale of your macramé project.
- Group fringe and tassels together: For a more cohesive look, group several strands of fringe or tassels together at the same point. This will create a more dramatic effect than individual strands scattered across the edge of your work.
- Experiment with texture and color: Don't be afraid to mix and match cord types or incorporate beads, shells, or other embellishments to create visual interest and depth.
- Trim with care: Once your fringe or tassels are in place, be careful not to trim them too short. A slightly uneven trim can add character and natural beauty to your work.

Fringes and tassels enhance the kinetic energy of life, adding an interactive dimension to our work. Whether it's a gentle sway in a peaceful breeze or the dynamic twirl in the midst of celebration, these elements capture the essence of movement, inviting touch and admiration. Experiment, enjoy the process, and watch as your knots transform into magical, mesmerizing masterpieces. Grant yourself permission to tap into the richness of your imagination and uncover the opportunities that await you.

Chapter 5: Tips, Tricks, and Troubleshooting

As you deepen your macramé practice, you'll inevitably encounter some hiccups along the way. It's all part of the creative process. In this chapter, we'll untangle some of the most common challenges macramé artists face, from dealing with tangled cords to achieving the perfect tension. Think of this as your handy guide to navigating those little bumps in the road. Whether you're a beginner or a more experienced knotter, troubleshooting is an essential aspect of mastering any craft, and macramé is no exception. So, let's get right to it and equip you with the tools to troubleshoot like a pro. Before you know it, you'll be knotting and creating with renewed confidence and ease!

5.1 Dealing with Tangled Cords

Let's tackle the knotty affair head-on. Finding yourself amidst a pile of spaghetti-like cords is no picnic. It's like trying to untangle a ball of knitting yarn after your cat has had a go at it! I can confidently say that we have all faced the challenge of entangled cords at one point or another. It's practically a rite of passage! However, untangling them doesn't have to be a headache or a time-consuming task. With the right techniques, patience, and a gentle touch, you can overcome this snarled setback.

Let's begin by addressing the issue of prevention, as it is indeed better than cure. To minimize the likelihood of your cords intertwining in the first place, be mindful of your work area. Keep your cords neatly organized, separate, and with adequate space between them during the crafting process. If you're working with lengthy cords, consider securing them with a clip or looping them around a rod to avoid unnecessary tangling. Ensure that each cord is separated and free of existing tangles before you start. It's tempting to overlook this step when enthusiasm is running high, but taking a moment to lay everything out will save you headaches later. Next, as you knot, be mindful of your movements. Slow down to let each knot form naturally, without forcing or yanking the cords. Gentle but firm tension will help you avoid pulling the cords out of alignment and creating those troublesome knots. Also, working on a vertical surface can help gravity keep the cords separated and prevent them from tangling as much.

Now, should you find your cords hopelessly entwined despite your best efforts, let us turn to our handy rescue techniques. The first step in negotiating with your knotty adversary is to remain calm. Take a deep breath, and let's coax those cords back into compliance. Then let's identify the **type of tangle** you're dealing with:

- *The Bird's Nest*: This is the most common type of tangle, where your cord resembles a bird's nest, with loops and knots all over. It usually happens when the cord is left unrestrained and free to roam. Start by identifying the center of the nest and work your way outwards. Gently pull on the loose ends, and try to find a central strand to work with. Slowly tease out the knots, working in a circular motion.

- *The Knotty Mess*: You might find yourself facing a series of tight, intricate knots that seem impossible to untangle. This often occurs when your cord gets pulled or twisted during crafting. With intricate knots, patience is key. Use your fingertips to gently work on one knot at a time. Try to identify the path of the cord and carefully loosen each twist and turn.

- *The Spaghetti Tangle*: Imagine a plate of spaghetti, all twisted and intertwined. This tangle happens when your cord gets tangled with itself, forming long loops and convoluted twists. Focus on separating the long loops first. Carefully pull on one loop at a time, working your way through the twists. You might find it helpful to gently twist the cord in the opposite direction to loosen the tangle.

One of the most common causes of tangled cords is working with too many strands at once. It's easy to get carried away and before you know it, your cords are a twisted mess. To avoid this, try working with smaller groups of cords at a time. You can always add more cords later once you've established a solid foundation. If you do find yourself with a tangled mess, start by gently pulling the cords apart. Try to identify which cords are connected to each other and slowly work them apart. It can be helpful to lay the cords out flat on a table or the floor as you work. If the tangles are particularly stubborn, you can try using a crochet hook or a knitting needle to gently work the cords apart. Be careful not to pull too hard or you may risk damaging the cords.

Another common cause of tangled cords is working with cords that are not the same length. This can cause the cords to twist and turn as you work, leading to tangles and knots. To avoid this, make sure all of your cords are the same length before you start your project. If you do end up with cords of different lengths, you can try sorting them out by grouping them by length. This can help you identify which cords are connected to each other and make it easier to untangle them.

If you've tried all the above and come up against a particularly stubborn knot, don't despair; reversing a few steps in your pattern can sometimes be the most straightforward solution. Undo your recent knots until you reach the tangled area, and you'll likely have an easier time setting those cords free.

Be prepared to encounter pesky snags and loops that refuse to budge. In these situations, it's crucial not to force the cords apart, as doing so may damage or fray your material. For particularly unruly cords, you may be surprised to find that a light coating of conditioner, applied to the tangled segment, can help smooth the fibers and ease the process of untangling. Simply massage the conditioner gently, leave it for a few minutes, and rinse your cords before continuing.

If your cords are persistently prone to tangling, consider switching to a different material. Smoother fibers like nylon, satin, or certain cotton blends can help reduce friction and tangling. These cords may not have the same rustic appeal as jute or hemp, but they offer a frustration-free alternative.

Finally, if all else fails, you can always cut the tangled cords and start over. It's not ideal, but sometimes it's necessary. Just be sure to add a few extra inches to your new cords to account for the lost length.

Once you've successfully navigated the treacherous terrain of tangled cords, it's time to reorganize them. Fear not, for I've got you covered. Use a clothespin or paperclip to hold the work in place while you work. Proceed to weave the cords back into their rightful place. Now, to prevent any future disasters, give each cord an identity. You could assign them letters or numbers, whatever is most comfortable for you. Secure these determining factors with a small tie, so that they never lose their way again.

Bonus Tip - "Prevention is Better than Cure": To minimize the likelihood of tangled cords, follow this mantra: proper storage, careful handling, and keeping cords in their designated place. Trust me, your hands will thank you later.

Tangled cords may seem like a daunting challenge. Remember, take your time and don't force anything. With a gentle approach and these quick-fix techniques, you'll soon have your cords back under control. When you find yourself wrapped up in knots, approach it thoughtfully, untangle with care, and appreciate the experience as part of your growth. Each tangle you untie not only smooths out your current project but also knots up some new wisdom for the next.

5.2 Adjusting Tension for Perfect Results

Finding the perfect tension in your macramé work can be a bit of a tightrope walk, but it will give your knots a neat, uniform look and feel.

Too much tension and your work will pucker and twist; too little and your knots will be loose and sloppy. It's all about finding that Goldilocks zone – not too tight, not too loose, but just right.

The first thing to remember is that consistency is key. You want your cords to have a uniform tension throughout your project, or else it will look unprofessional and uneven. To help you maintain this consistency, try using the same amount of force for each knot. I like to imagine I'm giving each cord a gentle yet firm hug – not a bear hug, mind you, but more like a warm embrace.

Now, let's address a common issue: how do you know if your cords have the right tension? Well, it's a feel thing, varying depending on your cord's thickness and texture, the complexity of the knot, and even the desired look of your piece. Tension isn't static, it's a dynamic element you adjust throughout your project. Feel your knots. Look at them. Are they too loose, losing their shape? Tighten up. Are they straining, looking pinched? Relax a bit. It's all about finding the sweet spot, that perfect balance where your knots are secure but not stressed. For delicate designs with thin cord, a lighter touch is key. Chunky cord and bold knots? You can crank up the pressure a notch.

Lastly, it's important to recognize that cord tension can vary depending on the type of cord you're using. Natural fibers, like cotton and hemp, tend to be more forgiving than synthetic materials, which can be slippery and less predictable when it comes to tension.

A good rule of thumb – and index finger! – is to envision the final form of your knot. Are you aiming for crisp, defined lines? Maintain consistent tension throughout. Want a softer, more organic look? Allow for a bit of give, easing up on the pressure as you tighten the knot.

One way to fine-tune your tension is by practicing on a spare piece of cord or an old, discarded project. This will help you gauge how much force is needed and allow you to experiment with different tensions. Remember, it's all about finding your sweet spot. You'll know it when you feel it, and your macramé will thank you for it!

On the other hand, if you find yourself struggling with consistently loose cords, try this hack: before you start tying knots, give your cords a little twist. This will add some tension and help prevent the cords from becoming too loose throughout your project. And, as always, be mindful of your technique and apply a consistent amount of force for each knot.

One trick to help you gauge tension is to hold your work up to the light. With the right tension, you should see a consistent pattern of gaps between the cords. If the gaps are wonky or vary in size, it's a sign that your tension needs adjusting.

Another helpful hint is to periodically lay your work on a flat surface and give it a gentle shake. If your knots slide around easily, you may need to tighten up your tension a tad. On the other hand, if your work feels rigid and refuses to lie flat, you might be pulling those cords a bit too tightly.

Practice definitely makes perfect when it comes to tension. The more you knot, the more you'll develop a natural feel for the right amount of tension. So, don't be too hard on yourself if your first few attempts aren't quite right – keep at it and you'll soon find your rhythm.

And finally, don't be afraid to adjust as you go. Macramé is an art, and like all arts, it requires a bit of experimentation. So, if you feel a section is too tight or too loose, don't be afraid to undo a few knots and try again. Your patience will be rewarded with beautiful, cohesive work that you can be proud of.

5.3 When Cords Fall Short

A macramé project is a creative endeavor, a piece of work born from knots and dedication that becomes a personal treasure. Yet sometimes, the universe challenges us with a surprise quiz on resourcefulness. You're in the flow, tying, looping, and then it hits you — your cords are coming up short. You've measured thrice, you've planned your piece to the inch, but here you are, standing at the precipice of an unfinished masterpiece. First, take a gentle breath — it's not the end of the world, and definitely not the end of your macramé masterpiece, but an opportunity to infuse even more creativity into your work. There's a simple charm to solutions born of necessity. Macramé, an art of transformation, teaches us that imperfection often leads to unique beauty. So, what to do when your cords are too short?

First things first: assess the damage. How short are we talking? A few inches? A foot? The solution depends on the severity of the shortfall. For minor gaps, consider incorporating smaller knots or spacing them out a tad more to stretch those precious inches or adding beads or other embellishments to bridge the gap stylishly. This not only solves the problem but adds a unique touch to your piece.

If you're facing a more substantial shortfall, fear not! The art of joining cords is your new best friend. Prepare to discover the array of reliable knots that patiently await their turn to extend your cords effortlessly and ensure your project's continuity.

1. The **square knot**, a fundamental macramé knot, works wonders here. Simply overlap the ends of your old and new cords, ensuring they're aligned, and tie a square knot to secure them. Trim any excess, and voila – you're back in business.

2. Take the **overhand knot** — its function is as practical as they come: a quick twist of two cord ends, loop through and pull tight, and your cords are united once more. You can situate this humble knot strategically, maybe right next to another knot or a bead, where it can merge into the texture of your piece, almost invisible, but ever so reliable.

3. Then we have the brilliant magic **weaver's knot** — a seamstress's secret, a conjurer's concealment of the cord's end. This knot whispers of permanence, as it tucks the ends away, leaving only the slightest trace. With a flick of the wrist, two strings become one, extending your work without a visual break. It's a subtle feat, but one

that can make all the difference between a work that's finished and one that's flawless.

4. The **fisherman's knot** is a robust connection akin to a partnership of strength and durability, bearing the weight of your work while maintaining a flexible grace.

But what if you don't have any extra cord on hand? This is where your creativity comes into play. Consider adjusting your design to work with the amount of cord you have available. Maybe you can simplify the pattern or make your piece a bit smaller than originally planned. Sometimes, these limitations can lead to unexpected and beautiful results. Instead of viewing your short cords as a problem, see them as an opportunity to create a minimalist piece. Focus on clean lines, simple knots, and negative space. Finally, if your cord is waning and the end is nigh for your piece, creative cropping can save the day. Adjust the pattern, remove an element — improvise. It's your chance to stand out, turning what some might call a flaw into a masterpiece's focal point. In some cases, you may be able to salvage a project by unraveling and re-tying knots to use less cord. This can be a time-consuming process, but it's worth a try if you're really attached to the project.

When cords fall short, don't let your creativity fall short with them. What we once saw as the prescribed border of our art is but an illusion. The only true boundary is our willingness to adapt and reinvent. Take on the macramé challenge, pioneer new techniques, and observe the development of your craft evolve into something even more stunning than you could have ever envisioned.

5.4 Common Mishaps and How to Fix Them

As with any new skill, there's a learning curve, and you might encounter some challenges along the way. I've been in your shoes, and I remember how frustrating it can be to encounter obstacles that seem intimidating at first. Welcome to the stage of our macramé examination, where we tackle some common hurdles with easy solutions that will surely elevate your confidence and expertise. As much as macramé is about the beautiful art of knotting, it's also about figuring out how to smooth over the little snags and tangles we encounter along the way.

In this subchapter, I'll share some quick fixes and simple solutions to address common mistakes and mishaps. These tips will have you knotting like a pro in no time!

5.4.1 Cord Management

Fringe Cords Fraying or Splitting: To prevent fraying or splitting, apply a small amount of fray check solution or clear nail polish directly to the ends of the cords. This will seal the fibers and protect them from further damage. When it comes to trimming your fringe, always opt for sharp scissors. A clean, decisive cut ensures the fibers are less likely to split.

Cord Unravelling: Like with fraying, you can address unravelling by applying clear nail polish or fray check to the ends of the cords, creating a seal. For a more permanent fix, lightly melt the ends of the cords with a lighter. This will fuse the fibers and stop further fraying. If you're using natural materials, fabric stiffener or a drop of hot glue can effectively seal the ends. Alternatively, use a needle to re-thread any errant strands back into the main cord, securing them neatly in place. For additional reinforcement, you can employ a whipping stitch or an overcast stitch at the cord ends to enhance the durability and maintain the structure of your project.

Cords Twisting or Knotting Unevenly: Maintain a steady tension on the working cord to ensure even knotting. Be mindful not to pull too tightly or loosely compared to the other cords. Before initializing your knotting process, give the cords a good stretch to loosen them up; this pre-emptive measure helps prevent the cords from twisting or kinking mid-project. Practicing these steps consistently will help you achieve more uniform knots and a cleaner overall look.

Maintaining Straight Cords During Project Work: Secure the end of your cords with a suitable weight. This could be anything from a special cord weight to a simple household item that can serve the purpose. Doing so will apply consistent tension along the length of the cord, keeping it straight and manageable, reducing the likelihood of tangling and twisting.

Handling Cords that Tangle or Stick: Start by separating your cords into individual strands. Take each cord and roll it gently between your fingers; this action will help alleviate any static and stiffness. If tangling occurs during your work, patiently detangle them with your fingers or a pin, avoiding forceful pulls that may damage the cords.

Securing Loose Ends: When finishing your piece, the ends of your cords can sometimes seem unruly. To secure them, weave the tails back through the backside of your knots using a tapestry needle or a similar tool. This not only conceals loose ends but also helps reinforce the sturdiness of your work.

Combating Minor Shrinkage: Macramé pieces, especially those made from cotton or other natural fibers, may shrink slightly when wet. To account for this, you could prewash your cords before cutting them to the desired length. Then, work with them while they're slightly damp for more elasticity, or stretch and pin them out while they dry to retain the desired shape.

Dealing with Gaposis: This occurs when there's an unintentional gap in your work due to misalignment of knots. To fix this, work from the nearest edge and carefully adjust the knots along the row, redistributing the cord as evenly as possible until the gap is eliminated.

Using Variegated Yarn in Projects: When planning your project with variegated yarn, consider the color transition pattern and how it will align with your design. You can strategically plan your project to highlight the color changes in the yarn. If your goal is a harmonious and uniform look, be selective with the sections of cord you use, choosing those with similar color variations. This approach will give you the benefit of the variegated tones while maintaining a consistent color scheme throughout your work.

Repairing a Broken Cord: If you run into the unfortunate event of a cord breaking, don't panic. If possible, rethread and tie the broken ends together with a discreet surgeon's knot. Then, hide the fix by weaving the ends into the surrounding knots.

Uneven Fringe Management: If your project features a fringe that ends up uneven, don't stress. Lay the piece on a flat surface and comb through the fringe with a fine-tooth comb to align the fibers. Then use sharp fabric scissors to trim the ends evenly. Work slowly and in small sections to avoid cutting too much off at once.

Identifying Multiple Cords in Complex Projects: Label each cord at one of its ends using colored tape or markers. This color-coding technique will simplify the process of identifying and selecting the correct cord, particularly in designs that require you to work with cords sequentially or in specific patterns. This organizational method is invaluable in preserving the structure within complex projects and ensures a smooth workflow.

Managing Large Amounts of Cord Efficiently: When working with excess cord, it's best to roll it into balls to keep it organised and tangle-free. Secure these balls with rubber bands for easy access and control over the amount of cord you dispense. Using clothespins or clips, you can attach cords to a book or magazine to keep them orderly. Design your project layout in a way where each row hangs loosely, allowing you to focus on one row at a time without affecting the rest, maintaining a neat and manageable workspace.

Cord Organization When Pausing Work: Before taking a hiatus, neatly roll or gather your cords and fasten them securely with rubber bands or clips. By doing this, you prevent the cords from becoming entangled and will ensure that your setup is ready for action as soon as you return. This simple step can save significant time and reduce frustration, allowing you to pick up right where you left off.

Handling Metallic or Specialty Cords: Before working with these cords, it's recommended to apply a light coat of beeswax or to use tape on the ends to provide additional protection against fraying. When tying knots with specialty cords, exercise caution and gently pull each knot to avoid causing damage. Handling the cords with care can significantly extend the life of your project and preserve the integrity of the delicate materials.

5.4.2 Knotting Techniques and Tension

Knot Tension Too Tight: If your piece feels stiff because the knots are too tight, then it's time for a gentle massage. Working your piece over with your hands can loosen the fibers and create a little give in your work, resulting in a softer, more flexible finished product.

Loose Knots: Conversely, overly loose knots can lead to a floppy and distorted macramé piece. If you find your knots are too loose, rework them by tightening each knot from the row end nearest to the start of your piece. Pull the weaving cords firmly but gently until you reach the desired level of tightness.

Knots Slipping on Smooth or Silky Cords: The key to solving slipping knots is to reinforce them with a tiny dab of clear-drying fabric glue. Be cautious to apply only a small amount, as too much glue can cause the cords to become rigid and compromise the natural flow of your project. This will help knots stay in place without negatively affecting the overall flexibility of the cord.

Difficulty Tightening Knots: When knots are challenging to tighten, it can be hard to achieve the desired tension. making use of a crochet hook can provide the necessary leverage. Simply guide the hook through the knot and use it to help pull tight. This technique allows for a uniform tension across knots and can make the process less taxing on your hands.

Knots Lacking Firmness and Structure: To add firmness to your knots, lightly spray them with fabric stiffener or a mixture of diluted white glue. Proceed with a gentle hand to avoid over-stiffening. This will help the knots to harden slightly, providing them with the solidity required to maintain their shape and enhancing the overall appearance and durability of the item.

Keeping Knots Evenly Spaced and Aligned: Obtaining a neat and orderly appearance in macramé requires uniform spacing and alignment of knots. Use a ruler or other measuring tool to gauge the distance between knots for a consistent layout. For symmetrical patterns or designs, pre-measure and mark the cord positions before knotting. Check your work frequently with the ruler and adjust as necessary for even distribution.

Misaligned Rows and Crooked Patterns: When creating macramé pieces, it is easy to lose track of where you are in a pattern, especially for beginners. To prevent misaligned rows, place a marker or safety pin at the beginning of each row to help you keep track. This way, you'll always know where to start the next row. If you notice a crooked pattern forming, take a step back and review your work. Count the number of knots and ensure they match the pattern instructions. Often, a simple miscount can throw off the entire design. Use a ruler or measuring tape to check the spacing between your knots. Uneven spacing can contribute to a lopsided look.

Maintaining a Straight Line of Macramé Double Half-Hitch Knots: Producing a straight line of double half-hitch knots can be challenging if the cords shift during the process. Fix your cords to a sturdy, straight anchor point to hold them in place as you work. Avoid twisting or overlapping the cord unnecessarily when forming the initial half-knot. Regular tension checks should be performed to ensure each knot is uniformly tensioned, contributing to a straight and even line of knots.

Securing Your Work Effectively While Knotting: To prevent your work from moving around, use masking tape or painter's tape to hold down the loose ends onto your working surface. This secures your project in place, minimizes slips, and aids in applying consistent tension as you knot, thus promoting an even and professional finish.

Fixing Oversized Knots: If a knot is larger than its neighbors and stands out, you can sometimes reduce its size by working it tighter and pulling excess cord through to the next knot in sequence. This incremental adjustment, made across several following knots, can spread out the excess and minimize the discrepancy.

Remembering Knot Types: As a beginner, the variety of knots can be overwhelming. Don't hesitate to keep a cheat sheet handy, with pictures and notes on how to tie each knot. With time, muscle memory will kick in, and you'll be knotting without a second thought.

Uneven Macramé Edges: If you find that your edges aren't as straight as a ruler, it's likely due to inconsistent knot sizing. To prevent this, use a measuring tape or a ruler while knotting to ensure each segment is of uniform length. Consistent measurement is your ally in maintaining crisp, clean edges.

Strategic Use of Beads: If you're having trouble keeping your space knots even, integrating beads into your design can not only add a decorative element but also act as a spacer to ensure consistency.

Moreover, beads can cover up any accidental irregularity in your knotting.

Neatening Wavy Edges: If a series of knots is supposed to form a straight line but turns out wavy, try using a steamer on the piece. This can relax the fibers slightly, allowing you to gently manipulate them into a straighter line.

Achieving Loop Consistency in Projects: Use a piece of cardboard or a ruler as your guide or template for the loops. This ensures that all loops are of the same size, which is incredibly helpful for achieving a uniform and professional look in your finished project. Keep the ruler or cardboard handy for all loops to avoid any inconsistencies.

Achieving Knot Replication Accuracy: Consistency is paramount when creating multiple pieces meant to be identical, such as earrings or parts of a matching set, but achieving this manually can be challenging. To ensure uniformity, construct a jig out of a small board with strategically placed nails or pins. This customizable template supports the exact size and shape for replication and is particularly helpful when precision is key.

Replacing Knot Types for Enhanced Texture: Following a pattern's prescribed knots can sometimes result in a texture or appearance that doesn't align with your vision for the project. Feel free to substitute a knot type with another of a similar size if the outcome of the original knot isn't satisfactory. This customization allows you to introduce a unique textural variety to your work and can even help resolve any issues you may have with the specific knotting sequence, adding a personal touch to your creation.

Working with Dark Colored Cords: Knotting with darker cords can be a visual strain due to the low contrast between the cord and the background. Place a light-colored or white cloth behind your work area when using dark cords to enhance visibility. The contrast will illuminate the details of your knots, making them easier to see, manage, and execute with precision.

Enhancing Visibility for Light-Colored Cords: Knotting with light-colored cords can be just as trying as with dark ones due to the lack of contrast, which might obscure the details of your work. Lay a dark cloth on your working surface or your lap which will create stark contrast and improve the visibility of light-colored knots and cords.

Creating Clean Color Blocks with Knots: When creating a piece with distinct color sections, delineating sharp lines between colors can be difficult to achieve. Employ diagonal clove hitch knots for effective color blocking. This type of knot allows for precise and sharp or gradual transitions between colors, helping you achieve distinct, crisp color boundaries within your piece.

Concealing Unintentional Knot Mistakes: Mistakes in knotting are not uncommon and can stand out, particularly if they disrupt a consistent pattern. Creatively incorporate embellishments like beads or hoops into your design where knots haven't turned out as planned. These decorative elements can effectively mask imperfections, resulting in a seemingly intentional and enhanced design feature.

5.4.3 Design and Aesthetics

Keeping Track of Patterns: For complex patterns, maintaining the correct sequence can be bewildering. Keep a pattern guide or a numbered diagram near your workspace, and check off each row as you complete it. You can also use stitch markers or colored threads to mark your place.

Improving Symmetry in Doubles and Mirrors: When you're working with patterns that require symmetry, use your initial half as the template for the second. Use a tape measure to ensure that both sides are even. Regularly compare the matching sections by laying them out next to each other as you go. This helps to replicate the pattern accurately and maintain symmetry.

Dealing with Pattern Complexity: When working on a complex pattern with multiple repeating sections, consider using a highlighter or sticky notes to keep track of your progress on your pattern instructions. Highlight or mark off each section as you complete it to avoid losing your place.

Aligning Horizontal Bars: For patterns that involve a series of horizontal bars, like those created by the double half hitch, use a spirit level or a straight edge to check that the bars are level as you go. This will ensure a polished final appearance.

Ensuring a Professional Finish: Spend time on the finishing touches of your work. Steam or iron flat components, trim fringes evenly, and use a needle to hide any loose ends on the backside of your work.

Regularly Step Back: It's easy to get engrossed in the details and lose sight of the overall design. Frequently step back from your work to view the piece as a whole from a distance. This provides perspective on the balance and symmetry of your project and allows you to catch any irregularities early on.

Managing Cord Supply for Long Projects: If you're knee-deep in a large project and are concerned about running out of cord, order more from the same dye lot as early as possible to ensure color consistency. If you cannot get the exact match, introduce the new cord subtly into the piece to minimize any disparity.

Combating Cord Yellowness: If you're using white or light-colored cords that have turned yellow or dingy over time, try soaking the cords in a mixture of water with a bit of hydrogen peroxide. This can help brighten them up, but be sure to patch test first to ensure the cords can handle it.

Preventing Fading: To prevent fading in macramé pieces exposed to sunlight, use UV protectant spray suitable for fabrics. This can help prolong the vividness of dyed cords.

Final Inspection and Adjustment: Once your piece is complete, give it a thorough inspection. Look for any loose knots, uneven tension, or stray cords. Make fine adjustments to perfect its appearance. Sometimes, these minor tweaks can significantly enhance the aesthetics of your macramé creation.

Correcting Uneven Tension after Completion: If you notice some areas with inconsistent tension after your piece is finished, you may be able to wet the entire piece and lay it on a flat surface to dry. While damp, you can manipulate the knots to evenly redistribute the cord and even out the tension throughout the work.

Reframing Mistakes as Design Choices: Sometimes, even with your best efforts, mistakes happen, and they're often difficult to undo. Rather than seeing this as a setback, view it as a creative opportunity. Repurpose these mistakes as intentional design elements, marking your piece with a personal touch.

Color Coordination Conundrums: Sometimes what looked like a harmonious color palette in theory translates differently in practice. If the colors in your piece don't blend as hoped, you can subtly shift the aesthetic by adding more of a dominant color or incorporating neutral tones that bridge the mismatched colors together. For example, adding shades of beige, white, or grey can sometimes neutralize overly bold contrasts, bringing a more cohesive feel to your piece.

5.4.4 Project Planning and Finishing

Managing Workstation Organization: Keep your workspace well organized. Use hooks or dowels to hang cords and keep different lengths easily accessible. This not only streamlines your workflow but also prevents your cords from becoming entangled or dirty.

Maintaining a Clean Working Environment: Fibers from macramé cords can accumulate and create a mess on your workspace. Regularly clean the area with a lint roller to pick up any stray fibers. Keeping your workspace clean helps prevent these fibers from getting tangled in your project.

Creating a Stiff Foundation: When beginning a piece, especially one that requires straight lines at the start like a wall hanging, use a stiff piece of cardboard cut to the desired width as a temporary base. Tie your initial row of knots onto the cardboard. Once the foundation is sturdy enough, you can remove the cardboard and continue with your work.

Visual Cue for Measurements: For repeated measurements, instead of using a ruler every time, use a piece of tape on your work surface to mark the length. This quick visual cue can streamline the process and save time.

Non-Slip Work Surface: Work on a non-slip mat or surface to prevent your project from sliding around, which can affect knot consistency and make the process more cumbersome.

Dealing with Workspace Limitations: If your crafting area isn't large enough to lay out your work flat, use the vertical space. Hang your work on a wall or door using a dowel and S-hooks, which allows you to step back and assess your piece in progress with ease.

Cord Strength Testing: Before starting a new type of project, like a plant hanger, test the strength of your chosen cord with the intended weight. This ensures that your finished piece will be both beautiful and functional.

Bundling Projects for Efficiency: If you have multiple pieces to work on, consider bundling projects that use the same knot types. This allows you to get into a rhythm with a specific knot, potentially speeding up your overall process.

Curved Work when You Want it Straight: Sometimes larger macramé pieces start to form a curve when you've planned for a straight design. This can be a result of variable tension. Consistent tension is key. You might consider using a weighted object to maintain even tension and keep your work straight, especially on wider pieces that are more prone to curving. A loom can be invaluable here, anchoring points across the width of your work.

Your Macramé Piece is Too Heavy or Bulky for The Dowel: For larger and heavier macramé pieces, consider using stronger anchor points like wooden dowels, metal rods, or even DIY PVC pipes. These materials can withstand more weight and prevent warping or sagging. To further support heavy or bulky macramé projects, use multiple dowels or rods and space them at intervals throughout the length of the piece. Securing the cords at multiple points will distribute the weight evenly and keep your project flat and stable.

Ensuring Your Macramé Projects' Finished Edges Are Secure and Unravelling: Consider incorporating decorative edge knots such as a support knot or a picot stitch to secure the ends and add visual interest to your piece. Use a needle to weave any loose ends under the completed rows, securing them in place and creating a finished edge with a neat and flat appearance.

Adjusting for Environmental Factors: Unexpectedly, environmental factors like humidity and temperature can affect your working material. If you're working in a particularly damp or dry environment, your cords might react by contracting or expanding. Be mindful of where you store your materials and try to work in a controlled environment when possible. If your indoor climate is variable, consider pre-conditioning your cords to the working environment before beginning your project to minimize adjustments later on.

5.4.5 Advanced Techniques

Restoring Color Vibrancy in Dyed Cords: Sunlight and handling can cause colored cords to fade or look a bit dingy. If you notice your project has lost some of its luster, you can carefully hand-wash it using a mild detergent and lay it flat to dry. This can help brighten up the colors. Be sure to test a small, inconspicuous area first for colorfastness.

Preventing Color Bleed in Dyed Cords: Before working with dyed cords, especially deep or vibrant colors, you can pre-soak and rinse them until the water runs clear to reduce the risk of color bleeding later on. Always allow cords to dry completely before using them in your project.

Conclusion

Our journey together has come full circle, and I couldn't be more proud to see how far you've come! *"The Essential Guide to Macramé for Beginners"* has been your trusted companion, guiding you through the fundamentals, and empowering you to create stunning handcrafted home decor and gift ideas.

As we draw this chapter, and indeed this book, to a close, I wanted to take a moment to reflect on all that we've covered. We began with an overview of macramé's rich history and the reasons behind its resurgence in popularity today, diving deeper into the art of creating a comfortable and functional workspace before moving on to selecting the perfect cords for our projects. We then learned about essential tools and material characteristics, mastered cord lengths and measurements, and perfected finishing techniques. Throughout our time together, we've also examined Macramé's versatility in adding texture, dimension, and flair through beads and fringes.

Above all else, it's been my goal that by the time you reach the end of this guide, you feel empowered to create beautiful and unique macramé projects. You are now armed with knowledge about knots and techniques that will allow you to tackle any piece of home decor or handmade gift with confidence. From the Lark's head knot to adding fringes and beads, you are now a true macramé connoisseur. But perhaps most importantly, you understand the importance of taking your time, embracing the craft's therapeutic nature, and making mistakes along the way.

I truly believe that anyone can learn Macramé. It's about embracing imperfection and finding joy in the process of creation. With patience, dedication, and practice, even the trickiest of knots will soon become second nature. Don't be afraid to experiment with colors, textures, and patterns - these are what make your work truly special. Remember that macramé is a timeless art form that has stood the test of time, and by incorporating these timeless elements, you'll be adding beauty and functionality to any space. Whether you plan on hanging your pieces as home decor or gifting them to loved ones, rest assured that each creation you bring into existence will be treasured.

You now hold the power to transform simple cords into exquisite masterpieces. The techniques and tips you've learned will serve as your foundation, but it is your unique creativity that will set your handcrafted creations apart. As you master the basics of macramé and create stunning pieces, it's imperative to stay inspired and keep evolving in your craft. Surround yourself with inspiration - follow other macramé artists on social media, attend workshops, and experiment with new techniques and patterns. Never hesitate to seek inspiration from nature, as it's the purest form of creativity. Observing the textures and forms found in nature can inspire intricate patterns and designs that will elevate your work. And don't forget to share your creations! Share them with friends and family, display them proudly in your home, or give them as gifts to spread joy and warmth. Whatever you do, know that your handmade pieces are infused with love, care, and a piece of yourself, making them truly unique and precious.

As you look back on the magnificent creations you've crafted, I hope you're reminded of the joy and satisfaction that comes from fostering something from start to finish, piece by piece, stitch by stitch. The tactile experience of working with cord, the sensory delight of watching your creation take shape, and the sense of pride in knowing that you made it with your own two hands – these are the moments that make macramé so special.

Now, as you venture into the next chapter of your macramé adventure, I want you to remember that mastering this art form is a continuous process. Continuously adapting, learning, and refining your skills. I encourage you to stay curious, keep experimenting, and never be afraid to try new things; that's where true growth and creativity happen. Keep in mind, your macramé endeavor is special to you, and there are no limits to what you can create. Keep pushing yourself, stay inspired, and let your imagination run wild. The more you experiment and challenge yourself, the more your skills will grow, and your macramé creations will become even more extraordinary. This isn't the end of the road; it's just beginning.

Lastly, never underestimate the power of your own creativity and potential. Believe in yourself, take calculated risks, and trust the magic that happens when you combine your vision, passion, and skills.

Remember, every cord has a story to tell, and every macramé piece holds a special place in someone's heart.

As you turn the final page and begin to tie off the last knot in this literary macramé, know that my support and encouragement stay with you like a gentle breeze at your back. I can't wait to see each of your creations blossom, just as you have bloomed as an artist throughout your macramé journey. Keep shining your light, creating, growing, and sharing your love for macramé with the universe. I'm sure your macramé endeavors will be marked by thrilling discoveries, challenging periods, and achievements that bring you immense fulfillment. And now, as the ink on these pages dries, and the last cord has been knotted, it's time to let your creativity take flight. The world is your displayed wall space, and the sky is the knot-y limit!

Unlock the Power of Macramé
Get Instant Access to Your Exclusive Bonuses

https://alexandradixonjackson.emporiumbookstore.com/47906/bonuses
book

By scanning the QR code (or going to the link) above, you'll gain exclusive access to an incredible collection of online resources to help you take your macramé skills to the next level.

Scan the QR code now and unlock your bonus package!

Made in the USA
Las Vegas, NV
09 December 2024

13738500R00087